THE YOUNG, THE RESTLESS, AND THE DEAD

Film and Media Studies Series

Film studies is the critical exploration of cinematic texts as art and entertainment, as well as the industries that produce them and the audiences that consume them. Although a medium barely one hundred years old, film is already transformed through the emergence of new media forms. Media studies is an interdisciplinary field that considers the nature and effects of mass media upon individuals and society and analyzes media content and representations. Despite changing modes of consumption—especially the proliferation of individuated viewing technologies—film has retained its cultural dominance into the 21st century, and it is this transformative moment that the WLU Press Film and Media Studies series addresses.

Our Film and Media Studies series includes topics such as identity, gender, sexuality, class, race, visuality, space, music, new media, aesthetics, genre, youth culture, popular culture, consumer culture, regional/national cinemas, film policy, film theory, and film history.

Wilfrid Laurier University Press invites submissions. For further information, please contact the Series editors, all of whom are in the Department of English and Film Studies at Wilfrid Laurier University:

Dr. Philippa Gates
Email: pgates@wlu.ca

Dr. Russell Kilbourn
Email: rkilbourn@wlu.ca

Dr. Ute Lischke
Email: ulischke@wlu.ca

Department of English and Film Studies
Wilfrid Laurier University
75 University Avenue West
Waterloo, ON N2L 3C5
Canada
Phone: 519-884-0710
Fax: 519-884-8307

VOLUME **1**

THE YOUNG, THE RESTLESS, AND THE DEAD

INTERVIEWS WITH CANADIAN FILMMAKERS

EDITED BY GEORGE MELNYK

Wilfrid Laurier University Press

[WLU]

We acknowledge the support of the Canada Council for the Arts for our publishing program. We acknowledge the financial support of the Government of Canada through its Book Publishing Industry Development Program for its publishing activities.

LIBRARY AND ARCHIVES CANADA CATALOGUING IN PUBLICATION

The young, the restless, and the dead : interviews with Canadian filmmakers / George Melnyk, editor.

(Film and media studies series)
ISBN 978-1-55458-036-1

1. Motion picture producers and directors — Canada — Interviews.   2. Motion pictures — Canada — History.
I. Melnyk, George   II. Series.

PN1993.5.C3Y68 2008   791.430971   C2008-900393-4

© 2008 Wilfrid Laurier University Press
Waterloo, Ontario, Canada
www.wlupress.wlu.ca

Cover design by Blakeley Words+Pictures. Cover photograph by Valentin Casarsa / iStockphoto.com. Text design by Pam Woodland.

Every reasonable effort has been made to acquire permission for copyright material used in this text, and to acknowledge all such indebtedness accurately. Any errors and omissions called to the publisher's attention will be corrected in future printings.

This book is printed on Ancient Forest Friendly paper (100% post-consumer recycled).

Printed in Canada

The young, the restless, and the dead: An introduction **George Melnyk vii**

THE YOUNG

THE RESTLESS

THE DEAD

■

The interview as an interrogatory form of research has both advantages and disadvantages. The advantages include the pleasure of reading spontaneous expressions of orality,[1] the revelation of personal experience that has not been part of the record, a strong sense of the interviewee's form of speech, insight into the evolution of a project—often missing in critical discourse on completed works of art—and the presence of a vital emotional response to issues that can be a mainstay of the interviewee's professional life but exhibited nowhere else.

The disadvantages are equally numerous. Some interviewees are evasive and hesitant, while others are outgoing and unafraid to express their feelings and viewpoints. This means some interviews are captivating, others less so. Interviews can range from rambling and almost incoherent to so precise and defined that one senses barriers more than anything else. Some interviewers are "professional" in the sense that they can evoke responses that are truly enlightening, while others are more amateurish and so elicit less insightful answers. Some interviews display a genuine camaraderie between the interviewee and the interviewer, while others seem like formal Q&A exercises. Also, an interview is very much of the moment. Like a photograph, it captures a particular point in time and space that an interviewee has inhabited. An interview done the next day, by a different interviewer, for a different publication could result in something completely different. This means that there is the quality of the ephemeral that creeps into an interview and colours it. As a result, the typology of interviews occupies a wide and sometimes chaotic range that can make standardization of the form difficult and, in the end, not really worthwhile.

Most of us experience the interview through journalism. We read interviews in newspapers, trade or professional magazines, or on the Web. Occasionally interviews appear in books, either on their own or as addenda to critical studies. Most often, interviews serve as simply the raw material of research, reappearing as occasional quotes or paraphrases to support an argument or an insight. I have chosen to feature the interview as a valid interlocutory statement in its own right, useful to scholars and non-scholars alike. Believing that the Canadian filmmaker needs to be known through his or her eyes as much as through the eyes of the critic, I have launched this series of interviews with the hope that scholars and the public will have access to creators of cinema in a format that is readily available, whenever required. Books are easy to save and store.

The title of this book (and the series), *The Young, the Restless, and the Dead*, requires an explanation. The Young refers to filmmakers who are generally under forty and have just launched their careers with one or two feature films. They represent the future of the Canadian film industry. The Restless are those filmmakers of any age who have established themselves in the field with a body of work recognized by their peers and critics alike. They are the present, which forms the backbone of the contemporary creative canon. The Dead are those deceased filmmakers who have come to be acknowledged as significant figures in the field and whose work continues to inspire and attract critical acclaim. The former two categories are filled with original interviews for this book, while the latter category is based on previously published material.

Each volume in this series will contain from eight to ten interviews that vary in length from 3,000 to 6,000 words each. The choice of interviewees will be eclectic, while the interviewers will be primarily academic. The scholars that have been selected to do the interviews have a background in the filmmaker's work and bring a critical approach to their questions and discussion. Media interviewers are often less knowledgeable and have goals other than that of gaining insight into the filmmaker's work, which is the main purpose of this book. In general the interviews begin as audio tapes or as e-mail responses to questions. The audio tapes are transcribed verbatim and the resulting interview material is edited by the interviewer to a suitable length. This draft is edited by the editor of the book and then reviewed and revised by the interviewee so that the final result reflects his or her responses to the questions asked. Why these stages? The goals are accuracy and readability, and this process is necessary to achieve both ends. The document that emerges from this process provides material "for the record." In confirmation of this goal the editor intends to create a university archive of the interviews in the series that would contain the audio tapes, original e-mails, and various versions of the interviews so that future researchers into Canadian cinema are able to follow and analyze the process.

This volume begins with an interview in **THE YOUNG** category. It's with **Michael Dowse**, who was born in London, Ontario, in 1973. He moved to Calgary, where he went to school and graduated from the University of Calgary. He made his first auteur debut with *FUBAR* in 2002. F.U.B.A.R. is the urban lingo acronym for "Fucked Up Beyond All Reason" or "Fucked Up Beyond All Repair," and the film is self-described as "the original banger classic" on its Web site. Set in Calgary, the film deals with the antics of a couple of alienated slackers. The film was a cult hit. Dowse followed this initial success several years later with his sophomore auteur film, *It's All Gone Pete Tong*, a Canada–UK co-production about a dance music DJ living and working on the Spanish island of Ibiza. Dowse, who currently lives in Montreal, represents the new globalized generation of Canadian film directors for whom there are no territorial boundaries in the creative consciousness. They are part of the great digital web of music, visual imagery, and subject matter. Bart Beaty, who teaches popular culture and communication at the University of Calgary, interviewed Dowse.

The second section, **THE RESTLESS**, is more diverse and includes three Canadian women filmmakers—Mina Shum, Lynne Stopkewich, and Anne Wheeler—as well as five males—Guy Maddin and Gary Burns, both interviewed by George Melnyk of the University of Calgary, and a troika who run Anagram Films of Vancouver.

The first interview is with **Blake Corbet, Andrew Currie,** and **Trent Carlson,** the principals of Anagram Pictures. They have begun making waves with several recent films. They are interviewed by Peggy Thompson, who teaches screenwriting at the University of British Columbia. Since Vancouver is one of the three major centres of film production in Canada, along with Toronto and Montreal, and a leading venue for American offshore productions, Anagram's vision for and experience of Canadian feature filmmaking provides a searching look into the industry today.

Anagram Pictures was founded in 1996 by Currie and Carlson. Corbet joined a couple of years later. Carlson is a graduate of the Simon Fraser University film program (1993). The company has made three notable films—*Mile Zero* (2001), *Delicate Art of Parking* (2003), and *Fido* (2006). Because the films tend toward the dark comedy genre, they represent an important Canadian approach to humour, which parallels the approach favoured by Dowse. It seems to be a generational leaning. These Generation X filmmakers have taken their cue from Vancouver's own Douglas Coupland, whose 1991 novel, *Generation X,* launched the term into popular north American vocabulary. This transitional generation—childhood in the 1970s, youth in the 1980s, early adulthood in the 1990s—eschewed the serious intents of the radical boomer generation for satire, mimicry, and self-deprecation.

The second interview is with **Guy Maddin,** who was born in Winnipeg in 1956 and lives there now. Known for his idiosyncratic black-and-white silent-era imitative films, Maddin launched his career in 1988 with *Tales from the Gimli Hospital,* a surreal tale set in Manitoba's Icelandic community on the shores of Lake Winnipeg. His second feature, *Archangel* (1990), was set in Russia at the end of World War One and was a homage to Russian montage. He then moved to German cinema, recreating a 1930s "mountain genre" film titled *Careful* in 1992. He made several more features (and shorts) before his 2003 release, *The Saddest Music in the World,* a tale set in Winnipeg during the Great Depression as various nationalities compete to win the prize for the saddest music in the world.

He then did an "autobiographical" film titled *Cowards Bend the Knee* (2004) and in 2003 published two books—*From the Atelier Tovar: Selected Writings* and *Cowards Bend the Knee*. In 2006 he premiered *Brand Upon the Brain* at the Toronto International Film Festival, a silent film that used a live orchestra for music.

As a filmmaker who has staked his career on Winnipeg, he concludes with a certain melancholy that "from a stationary position I churn thoughtlessly through my time spent here on Earth, past the vistas and the plains of my outer landscape—Winnipeg—a life lived with glacial slowness."[2] For someone who is going nowhere, he has certainly given Canadian cinema a whole new dimension and his films have an international cult following. In 2007 he moved to Toronto, suggesting his Winnipeg life may be over.

Mina Shum, who was born in Hong Kong but raised in Vancouver, where she still lives, made her first film, *Picture Perfect*, in 1989. She did not make waves on the cinema scene till 1994, however, with *Double Happiness*, which she wrote and directed and acted in. This autobiographically based look at Chinese immigrant family life in Canada was considered a breakthrough. She followed its success with *Drive, She Said* (1997), and *Long Life, Happiness and Prosperity* (2002), both of which she wrote and directed.

As an auteur filmmaker, Mina Shum has opened the Asian persona to a wide audience and revealed the challenges and contradictions of multi-generational family life in Canadian society. Although she has worked extensively in the Vancouver television industry, it is the clash of Old World and New World values that is a mainstay of her feature films. She is interviewed by Jacqueline Levitin from Simon Fraser University.

Lynne Stopkewich was born in Montreal in 1964. Her debut feature, *Kissed* (1996), was a serious treatment of transgressive love. Based on a short story titled "We So Seldom Look on Love," by renowned Canadian novelist Barbara Gowdy, the film explores the consciousness of a necrophile who works in a funeral home in Vancouver. Stopkewich both wrote and directed *Kissed* when she was in her early thirties. Rather than adopt the Hollywood approach of using either comedy or horror genres to marginalize the topic, Stopkewich was distinctly Canadian in using drama as a vehicle. Her second feature, *Suspicious River* (2000), continued the discussion of female sexuality.

Since then she has made a music documentary (*Lilith on Top*, 2001) and directed television dramas. Just as Shum was able to use the Canadian actor Sandra Oh early in her film career, so Lynne used Molly Parker. Both women have gone on to major television careers in the US. Shum is interviewed by Kalli Paakspuu of York University.

Gary Burns (*b.* 1961) is a lifelong Calgarian who has made four feature films since the mid-1990s. His black comedy about Calgary's office-towers, *waydowntown* (2000), was awarded Best Canadian Feature at the Toronto International Film Festival. Trained in film at Concordia University, Burns began with two modest auteur productions—*The Suburbanators* (1995) and *Kitchen Party* (1997), which expressed the going-nowhere attitudes of Generation X youth. Critics considered these films as expressions of North American life because of Calgary's "American" attitudes and culture. After *waydowntown*'s success Burns made *A Problem with Fear* (2003), which was based on a similar downtown scene but was not well received. Yet he continued with his fascination with urbanity as represented by Calgary with the acclaimed mockumentary *Radiant City* (2006), co-produced with the National Film Board. The film savages suburban sprawl as exemplified by Calgary. While Shum and Stopkewich depend on female cultural grammars to convey their vision, Burns sees the world through the eyes of a male satirist.

Anne Wheeler (*b.* 1946) was born and raised in Edmonton, where she began as a documentary filmmaker. Her breakthrough feature was *Bye Bye Blues* (1989), starring Rebecca Jenkins, who won a Genie for Best Performance by an Actress in a Leading Role. The story was vaguely based on the life of her mother during the Second World War. Anne's father was a Japanese prisoner of war. Earlier Wheeler had done a docu-drama about her father's incarceration (*A War Story*, 1982). She had also directed and produced the 1986 made-for-television feminist drama *Loyalties* (1986), which told the story of a white woman and a native woman in northern Alberta. After the acclaim received for *Bye Bye Blues,* she did several youth-oriented feature films and went on to direct *Better Than Chocolate* (1999), a lesbian love story that received wide circulation in mainstream theatres. Two further features, which were primarily romantic comedies, came out early in the new century, but her bread-and-butter work continues to be in television, much as it is for Shum and Stopkewich. All three women directors work in the Vancouver-based industry. Wheeler approaches filmmaking as an art that recognizes the value of each character. "There are no villains in my movies," she has stated. "There are just people who make mistakes."[3] She is interviewed by Peggy Thompson of the University of British Columbia.

The final section, **THE DEAD**, contains an interview with the late **Jean-Claude Lauzon** (1953–1997), who was born in Montreal. He made only two feature films, but both were recognized as outstanding works. *Un Zoo La Nuit* (1987) won Best Motion Picture at the Genies as well as Best Screenplay (Lauzon) and Best Achievement in Direction. Lauzon followed his auteur debut with his masterpiece *Léolo* (1992), for which he again received a Genie for Best Original Screenplay. Both films deal with family relationships in a truly raw way with strong metaphors and disturbing imagery. The films are often driven by powerful music scores. The interview was done by Claude Racine and translated by Jim Leach of Brock University.

These seven interviews represent a wide range of directorial and screenwriting talent from Montreal to Vancouver. They capture the minds of Canadian filmmakers as they work to create national cinemas in a country whose film audiences have been Hollywood-ized and hostile to indigenous production. This is especially true in English Canada, where screen times for Canadian films average under 2 per cent annually and most films are relegated to the art house circuit. In Quebec since 2000, the situation has changed, with recent attendance for Quebec films in the 25 per cent range, which is a truly remarkable achievement. Canadian identity has benefited from its creative talent in a number of artistic fields. These interviews represent some of that talent and how it speaks for all of us.

NOTES

1   It is important for readers to realize that the "verbatim" interview is often a construct. For example, a two-hour interview can end up as a fifty-page double-spaced, raw document, unpublishable and barely readable in that form. This transcribed material has to be edited into coherent sentences and subject matter with more material deleted than retained. A published oral interview is a work of literacy, not orality.

2   Guy Maddin, *From the Atelier Tovar: Selected Writings* (Toronto: Coach House Books, 2003), 87.

3   Katherine Monk, *Weird Sex and Snowshoes and Other Canadian Film Phenonema* (Vancouver: Raincoast Books, 2001), 85.

PART i

THE YOUNG

Michael Dowse

MICHAEL DOWSE interviewed by **Bart Beaty**

■

Beaty How did you first get involved in the film scene in Calgary, and what role did that play in your formation as a filmmaker?

Dowse I started at the University of Calgary and worked at the University of Calgary television station (NUTV), which was a great place. I just basically found a place where they would rent you a camera cheap and had editing equipment. As long you volunteered on the show, and helped produce their half-hour show on cable television, you could basically use the equipment any way you wanted. So, I started there and then got involved with the CSIF (Calgary Society of Independent Filmmakers) which was sort of the graduation up to film, shooting off of 16mm. And so there were tons of good resources in Calgary where you could go to start learning. The influence of Calgary? It's kind of evident in *FUBAR*, you know, which is a take on something that's so Calgary to me, which is the headbanger.

Beaty Do you think that the headbanger is a particularly Calgarian thing?

Dowse I think that it's universal, but I think that Calgary provides some great examples and is a great breeding ground.

Beaty Are these the kind of guys that you met in university, or in high school in Calgary?

Dowse More like on jobs, and working in gas stations and playing against. Not necessarily in high school, more in junior high, I'd say.

Beaty When you made *FUBAR* it was edited at CSIF (Calgary Society of Independent Filmmakers). Did you borrow the equipment from CSIF as well?

Dowse The sound equipment we borrowed. We did all the sound, and all the sound editing, at CSIF.

Beaty The film was shot on DV [digital video]?

Dowse On mini-DV. And then the CSIF helped us out.

Beaty Was there a sense, growing up in Calgary or going to school in Calgary, that it would be a good place to make a film? Or did you have a feeling even then that you'd have to leave in order to make a career in film?

I started at the University of Calgary television station, which was a great place. I found a place where they would rent you a camera cheap and had editing equipment.

Dowse I knew eventually that I'd have to leave Calgary, but I think that it was a good place to make the first film because the community will help out. I didn't really want to get involved with the runaway American productions. In terms of staying in control behind the camera you kind of have to leave Calgary to really gain success. If you're just interested in working on a crew, I think that you can stay in Calgary. But that's definitely something that I wasn't interested in.

Beaty Was it difficult shooting in Calgary? Did you get permits, or did you just wander around downtown with the cameras?

Dowse We just wandered around. It was very easy to shoot in Calgary for that reason. We got no permits. I didn't really want to think like that at all on *FUBAR*.

Beaty Watching the film, I found myself trying to figure out exactly where the action is taking place at different moments. Some are very recognizable, like the LRT stations or the ice cream place on 17th Avenue. But otherwise, other than in the trip to High River, I'm not sure that the film really foregrounds the fact that it's set in Alberta. It could be set almost anywhere, and it's a more universal story that way.

Dowse Yeah, it could be. Actually, we shot most of it just behind 17th Avenue on 18th Street, where a giant condo development now sits.

Beaty Is that where you rented the house?

Dowse That's where we rented the house and we got it really cheaply because they were ripping it down. At the end of the day, they didn't really care what we did in there because they were going to rip it down. It was sort of a ritzy neighbourhood, but it works. You don't really notice the BMWs driving by. I think that one of the things that we missed out on was putting them in a duplex, but you can't have everything.

Beaty: Tell me a little bit about the trip to High River. I think that *FUBAR* has just about the greatest opening disclaimer in the history of film, which is the apology to people who thought you were making a real documentary, which is mostly the people in High River.

Dowse [*laughs*] Well, it was basically just a hot summer night. We were going to do a scene where Dean gets a hooker, and that's at the end of

> It had a certain danger to it that made it better in terms of the acting. Everyone went up a notch.

the night. But then we got there and we thought, "Oh, what the fuck, let's go out and start shooting and see what happens." It was either that or sit around for five hours waiting for it to get dark. And it was great. As soon as we turned on the camera people were genuinely interested. Literally, we shot for about five minutes walking around the town, when Paul Leonard, the guy who got attacked by the hawk, who told that story, just rolls up on his bike and says, "How you guys doing?" So it wasn't really a conscious artistic decision, just more of an idea that something interesting would happen if we embraced it and just went out and did something. And it had a certain danger to it that, I think, made it better in terms of the acting. Everyone went up a notch.

There wasn't a line scripted. We wrote out the narrative but we didn't script a line. The only scripted line was Dr. Lim's moustache joke at the end.

Beaty Generally, how much of the film was improv like that and how much was scripted?

Dowse Oh, there wasn't a line scripted. We wrote out the narrative but we didn't script a line. The only scripted line was Dr. Lim's moustache joke at the end. It was just something that I remembered us talking about in a meeting before we started shooting and I told him to say that line. It was a situation where we just wanted to make a movie and I didn't want to get involved at all with any of the infrastructure that always comes along with making a film. It was therefore a lot easier to shoot and you can just focus on getting the funny stuff.

Beaty What kind of ratio did you have on this film?

Dowse We shot about forty hours and then cut down to about seventy-eight minutes.

Beaty A lot of critics would suggest that the documentary, or even faux documentary, is a very Canadian style of filmmaking. Were you conscious of that as a Canadian influence, or was the influence more from films like *Spinal Tap*?

Dowse Well, first and foremost, it's an easy way to make a first film. But there's also a lot of great fake documentaries that I respect, like the Christopher Guest stuff. So I do have a genuine interest in working in that field, but it's also just the cheapest way to make a film. And we had no money, and we didn't want to get involved with trying to raise money for

We just wanted to make a movie and I didn't want to get involved with any of the infra-structure that comes along with that. It was therefore a lot easier to shoot and you can just focus on getting the funny stuff.

Paul Spence as Dean in *FUBAR* (2002): the 'banger in full glory. Photo: Alliance Atlantis Communications.

it. We thought that would just fucking slow it all down and we would end up never making this film. We would see ourselves three years later still trying to pitch this idea about 'bangers, which nobody would ever go for.

Beaty How much of the film came from Paul [Spence, "Dean"] and Dave [Lawrence, "Terry"]?

Dowse It's an equal split. I mean I think it's like a three-way split, the entire film, in terms of how we made it. It's a total partnership.

Beaty Did they come up with these characters before?

Dowse Dave had come up with Terry and Paul came up with Dean for the film. And they did a play for Loose Moose [a Calgary improv theatre company] before the film, just loosely working on developing the characters. And then we just went out and shot it. There was a lot of useable stuff there. I had a major hand in it as the editor as well as shooting it.

Beaty How long was the editing process?

Dowse About six months.

Beaty And how much did your conception of the film change over that time? I remember when I first saw the rough cut of it, it had a very different ending with Dean and Terry becoming the filmmakers after Farrell dies. Why did you change that?

Dowse Because the ending we went with was a better idea. I found the focus on Farrell to be distracting and not very funny, and sort of something that you don't really need to dwell on so much throughout the movie. It just worked much better that the story just moves along and that the film evolves from the idea that there's a guy beside the camera working and that it takes on its own perspective. You don't have to worry about who's shooting it, it's just enough that they are shooting now.

Beaty The film debuted at Sundance in January 2002. What was the reaction like there?

Dowse It was kind of crazy for us all. Nobody had been to a film festival that size and we had sixteen people from Calgary come crash with us. But audiences loved the film. It's really interesting when you go into that shark pit of acquisitions, because your hopes get up. And for us it

---

We just went out and shot it. There was a lot of useable stuff there.

was a situation where the film didn't have two stars, it's not very well shot, and its lack of an aesthetic is its aesthetic. Just watching the bald heads get up and walk out of the room after twenty minutes, but the other people stayed and were loving it.

Beaty Did you sell it in the States at Sundance?

Dowse No. We sold it a couple of months later to a kung fu distributor called Xenon. They also distribute Rudy Ray Moore films. I feel honoured to be under the same roof. But, no, we didn't sell it there. We came close, but no sales.

Beaty What happened to it after that? It was picked up for a couple of Canadian festivals.

Dowse It got picked up on the travelling thing that Toronto does. They screened it a few times. And it screened in a festival in Winnipeg. But it didn't do the circuit that year, because Toronto didn't accept it. Once Toronto didn't accept it, the distributor decided not to put it in anywhere else.

Beaty So the distribution in Canada wasn't a result of the festival circuit?

Dowse No. In Canada we had sold a rough cut to the distributor, which was one of the first things that we ever did. So it had a theatrical release and the size of it was helped by Sundance quite a bit. And it just sort of caught on and ran for six weeks, which was great. We sold the film on a rough cut, so we had used all our own money up to that point. The deal with the distributor unlocked some government money so we were able to do all the post work and distribution with those funds.

Beaty How crucial is the possibility of accessing government funding for a Canadian filmmaker?

Dowse It's horribly important. I think it's almost limiting for a Canadian filmmaker. It's great that it's there, but I think it breeds a different sort of producer who isn't necessarily as business savvy as you would want them to be. It also means that there's not really a marketplace accountability to the filmmaking in this country.

Beaty In *It's All Gone Pete Tong*, when the end credits roll up, there's the Canadian government, the BC government, the Movie Channel, and

> Government funding is horribly important. It's almost limiting for a Canadian filmmaker. It's great that it's there, but it breeds a different sort of producer who isn't necessarily as business savvy as you would want them to be.

all these funding agencies, but it's not really a very Canadian film in the classic sense. Was that a problem for them at all?

Dowse It was a co-production with England, so the Canadians were a minority participant, but we had the points to make it a Canadian film. Obviously it's not set anywhere near Canada, but there are a lot of Canadians involved in it, especially in the acting. They were genuinely hired on their talent, and not just to fill out CanCon [Canadian Content rules] points. All the sound was done in Canada, and the post, so it's involved.

Beaty How did *Pete Tong* come about? Was this the result of some British producers seeing *FUBAR* and thinking "this is the guy to make our club film in Ibiza!"?

In *It's All Gone Pete Tong*, the Canadians were a minority participant, but we had the points to make it a Canadian film.

Dowse Yeah. I went over to England to screen [*FUBAR*] at a festival and there I met these producers and they saw the film and my short film [*237*] and they made this proposition to me about doing a film in Ibiza. I wasn't really sure about what it was exactly, but they had a title and supposedly some money—which they did have. So that's how that film came about, and then I sort of went off and wrote a bunch of scripts.

Beaty Did you know a lot about European dance club culture before writing the script?

Dowse Not a thing. It's not really my bag. But I got to know the scene and did some research in London and met a lot of people. For me what was most important was figuring out the myth of the DJ and what the actual DJ does, and then trying to decipher that for people, so that people could understand the film and not be left on the outside looking in.

Beaty The film does a really nice job of establishing an authenticity about the culture through the opening title sequence, with the shots of Frankie on the cover of *Mixmag*—

Dowse And *Hello* magazine. That's my favourite detail that nobody notices!

Beaty I didn't notice *Hello* either!

Dowse It's at the very top of the opening and it goes by very quick, but he's in a *Hello* magazine spread, which was a very fun day to shoot.

Beaty The introduction of the various DJs—Paul Van Dyk, Carl Cox, and so on—credentials the character very quickly, but then you also move away from the fake-documentary sensibility. It's kind of a semi-fake documentary.

Dowse It's more like a fake bio piece because we're never interviewing any of the main characters. So the interviews work as narration and as comic relief as the story gets darker. Something that we played with in the edit suite was the amount of interviews used in the film, and it was something that I actually tested in some of the cuts that the producers did of the film. In some, there was just way too much use of it, basically as expository information that ended up killing the next scene. So the use of that kind of stuff was written into the script and it was a device to set up other scenes, but then when you shoot it, and you let the actors go with it a bit, you end up with a whole different set of nightmares. Then we ended up shooting more interviews to fill in some of the stories, but some of the performances just weren't great by some of the actors in the interviews. We did a mix, you know. We had some actors pretending to be authors or studio engineers, and we had actual famous people. We have a Boy George interview that I actually had to cut out. I cut Boy George out of my movie!

Beaty Did you script more of this film?

Dowse Completely. I completely scripted this film. But then we didn't follow the dialogue to a T when we shot it.

Beaty It has a lot of the same sort of energy as *FUBAR* does. I wonder if that's Paul Kaye's ["Frankie Wilde"] performance?

Dowse I don't know that it's just Paul's performance. Everybody brought a lot to it. Mike Wilmot ["Max Haggar"] has one of the most energized performances that I've seen in a long time. I love all the performances. Paul is sort of the background. He's got the weight of the film on his shoulders. But everybody, Mike Wilmot especially, out-energizes Paul by the end of the film. I always consider Mike to be a sort of B-52 that swings into the third act and makes it funny again.

Beaty In some of the discussion that I read about the film, particularly from British viewers, there was concern that the middle part of the film

> We have a Boy George interview that I actually had to cut out. I cut Boy George out of my movie!

is so dark when the trailers had promised a light comedy. Were you conscious about wanting to take this film into a really dark place?

Dowse I think that it needed to go to a dark place. I was interested in that. I think that comedy gets funnier if you take it really dark. Not that those dark periods are especially funny. But the film has a good range, I think, in terms of letting you take this character a little bit deeper.

Beaty It's definitely more of a character study than *FUBAR* is. How did you come up with some of the darker elements, like the coke badger for example?

Dowse The coke badger was an idea that came out of just wanting to personify his habit in a way that wasn't very preachy. It was just a visceral symbol of what his habit was like. It wasn't especially evil, in its way. The coke badger really evolved though. The audio was one of my favourite things to do. The audio was actually done by Gord Skilling, who played Farrell Mitchner in *FUBAR*. We brought him to Vancouver into an ADR booth and just played the scenes over and over again and got him to rant Portuguese gibberish and then we put it through a synthesizer filter to cut it up. So the coke badger really evolved. But I've always liked movies that played with the imagination of the main character.

Beaty I thought that the use of sound with the coke badger was really interesting, because it's hard to make out what he's saying, and that puts you in touch with what Frankie is feeling when he can never understand any of the other characters. So it plays off the major theme of not being able to hear properly.

Dowse It's just nonsense. The score that Graham Massey did for those scenes is sort of a psycho-billy wail of noise going on. I think that there's actually an elephant roar in the middle of it. At first we got real badger sounds off the Internet. But it was never really a conscious decision that the badger didn't make intelligent sounds, or that it would help your perspective on Frankie's problem.

Beaty Was the experience of shooting this very different from shooting *FUBAR*? Being in Ibiza? *FUBAR* is very much about a city that you grew up, and this Spanish island is really alien to your own experiences.

> The coke badger was an idea that came out of wanting to personify his habit in a way that wasn't preachy. It was just a visceral symbol of what his habit was like.

Dowse It's completely different. Both locations inform both films. But Ibiza is nuts. I think that a lot of the energy that's in the film is a direct reflection of some of the environments that we were shooting in. Some of these clubs are insane. We would have these grandiose plans to go in and shoot them, and then we'd get there and it would be 2,000 people on acid, so you're not going to be able to do anything, so you sort of do what you can.

Beaty I love when the crowd uses the giant Scrabble tiles to spell out "Frankie Wilde."

Dowse That's a great detail that you bring up, because that was a great night where everything just fell into place. We had no plans to use the Scrabble pieces until at the club I ran into this girl who we had used in one of the boat scenes, and she worked as one of these girls who would go around with these Scrabble pieces and they spell out anything—the name of the acts that are going on, the name of the DJ, anything. So I said "Can you spell this?" and I wrote it out for her. At 5:05 that night Frankie was to come down from the rafters and that would just be part of the show, so I asked that when that happens could she have her friends spell out his name. That was the moment when me and the DOP were like, "We sold it! We sold it!" with the big flaming M and the people going wild, it was fucking nuts. Paul coming down, it was perfect.

Ibiza is nuts. A lot of the energy that's in the film is a direct reflection of some of the environments that we were shooting in.

Beaty That was filmed in Manumission?

Dowse Yeah, it was filmed in Manumission, which is the biggest club in the world. There were 8,000, 9,000 people in there. We did a week of club scenes, and that was sort of our triumph. We did that one last. That club was fantastic to work with, and they gave us all the access that we wanted.

Beaty What was the reaction to *Pete Tong* in the UK?

Dowse Oh, they hated it.

Beaty It opened on more than 200 screens, which is a huge release there.

Dowse Oh, sure. They gave it the full ramp-out in the UK, but the poster made it look like a yoga movie. Terrible. Cross-legged. I hated the poster. No, they gave it the ol' college try and it did not succeed.

Beaty Did it do better in Canada and the United States? It got a great review in the *New York Times*.

Dowse It got great critical response in the States, but it's impossible to make an impact in that market without really strong word of mouth and a ton of money. So, they tried it there. It did better in Canada, where they did it with ten prints and a much smaller release and it did quite well. But in the other markets where they tried to go out with fifty prints, I guess it's just not that sort of film.

Beaty Was it a big victory for you to win Best Canadian Feature at Toronto after they had turned *FUBAR* down?

Dowse [*laughs*] It was great. Fantastic. I'll take that any day. It was great to have a certain acceptance of it, which is great, and a total surprise. I did not even think about that potential to win that award.

Beaty In terms of relating the two films to each other, one of the central motifs in each of your movies is that the main character gets seriously ill. Why the interest in making your characters face illness?

Dowse Because they're great stories to produce humour out of, and they make you care about the main character. It's sort of "plot in a bottle" in terms of thinking, "What's the worst thing that I can do to my main character?" and let's explore that and see what happens with that. The answer's as simple as that. You get to find the comic elements of sympathy.

Beaty Finally, there's a long tradition in writing about Canadian film to argue that the heroes of Canadian films are often losers. Do you think that your films fit this kind of trajectory of Canadian cinema, or is that just an easy out?

Dowse I don't know. I haven't really thought about whether the characters are losers. I guess that's true about a lot of Canadian films, but I don't know if I'd call Frankie a loser though. He's a winner at the end. And so is Deaner at the end. He's sort of a loser who wins.

Beaty Do you think Dean learns anything by the end of that film?

Dowse Yeah, but in a 'banger way, not in a sentimental way. We're exploring the idea of a sequel—whether or not Deaner's actually learned anything from the experience. Exploring that idea is just a way for us to

They gave it the full rampout in the UK, but the poster made it look like a yoga movie. Terrible. Cross-legged. I hated the poster.

keep the joke going, and give people exactly what they want, which is more nut cancer. We'll go after his other nut. Do it around Christmas and really play with people's emotions. I'd like to really push it to a story about a guy dying, where he loses his second nut and then drinks himself to death. What would happen to a 'banger with no nuts? He'd go crazy. A modern-day eunuch.

Beaty Is this the next project?

Dowse No, but we have a milder version of that that we'll be developing down the road.

Beaty Your career has taken off very quickly—from making a film with your own money, not being accepted into Toronto, to winning the award with your second film and going international. To what do you attribute that rapid success?

Dowse Always making a film, and keeping working, I guess. I don't know. Taking advantage of my opportunities and not getting stuck in that development hell where people expect to get a lot of money to make their films. *Tong* was originally supposed to be a half-million-pound budget [about $1.2 million CAD in 2006], but the realities of shooting a film in Ibiza made it much more expensive. Some people seem to think that they should be making a $3- or $4-million film right off a short film. But I think it's important to take advantage of opportunities that present themselves and not be concerned with getting paid a lot. *FUBAR* was self-made, and *Tong* was by no means sort of a hand-off, here you go. I had to write tons of scripts and tons of drafts. It was interesting working in a much more businesslike environment where they cared about the box office, about making it good, and where I had to meet a certain standard to even have a shot at it. But I think that a lot of people aren't interested in making films for even half a million Canadian dollars, where you can. The best way to become a director is to keep on working and shooting stuff.

Beaty Is there a Canadian sensibility that you see infusing your films?

Dowse There's a Canadian sense of humour that infuses them, for sure. An outsider's take on things. Sort of a sardonic look at subcultures.

It's important to take advantage of opportunities that present themselves and not be concerned with getting paid a lot.

Beaty I was going to say ironic. Although the end of *Tong* seems so sincere, maybe post-ironic. It's very heartfelt.

Dowse [*laughs*] I killed off the deaf lady in my edit, so I had a much different take. I'd read reviews and people would say "Oh, it ended so sympathetically" but I had much better plans for that. But I don't know if we want to go anywhere "post." What did you say?

Beaty Post-ironic.

Dowse Post-ironic. Fuck no. Not post-ironic. Not post-anything.

■

PART ii

THE RESTLESS

Blake Corbet

Andrew Currie

Trent Carlson

Guy Maddin

Mina Shum

Lynne Stopkewich

Gary Burns

Anne Wheeler

CORBET, CURRIE, CARLSON

the boys from **Anagram Pictures** interviewed with an introdution by **Peggy Thompson**

■

Anagram Pictures is a unique hybrid. On one hand, it's a collective of filmmakers who work on each other's films; on the other hand, it's a company that is making a big imprint on the Canadian film scene. Anagram's films have screened in theatres, in festivals, and on television around the world. Anagram's films share a commitment to storytelling, impeccable craft, and an exploration of what it is to be a man in a world in flux.

Anagram Pictures was founded in Vancouver in 1996 by filmmakers Andrew Currie and Trent Carlson. Blake Corbet joined the group in 1998. Anagram is dedicated to the development, financing, and production of "original, ground-breaking feature films for theatrical release around the world which promote social conscience and innovation." Anagram's roster to date includes the feature films *Mile Zero* (2001), *The Delicate Art of Parking* (2003), and *Fido* (2007). *Mile Zero* received very positive critical response in *Hollywood Reporter*: "An engrossing, low-key thriller featuring a riveting performance by Michael Riley in the lead role." Directed by Andrew Currie and produced by Trent Carlson and Blake Corbet, the film concerns an alienated father who kidnaps his young son on the pretense that they're going on a camping trip. The film tracks the father's emotional collapse and explores with style and depth the themes of fatherhood, masculinity, and contemporary paranoia. *Mile Zero* was well received critically, and put the group on the map.

The Delicate Art of Parking (2003) followed two years later. It is the story of a man who loves his job, and can tell you why. The film is a mockumentary about the people who issue parking tickets. It manages to incorporate elements of romance, mystery, heartbreak, determination, and friendship, according to Liz Braun (Jam! Movies), and be a good laugh. Anagram's first comedy was written and directed by Trent Carlson and was produced by Corbet and Currie. The film ran for months and attracted an almost cult-like following.

The company has grown. There are more partners, including producer Mary Anne Waterhouse (*Desolation Sound*), and more films. The most recent is *Fido*, Currie's zombie comedy, which was produced by Corbet. Corbet's own film, *Elijah*, about Aboriginal activist and politician Elijah Harper, for CTV, is well under way. However, the group still works together on each other's screenplays, hammering out ideas in their writers' room. And they all share the vision that film can serve to rattle the status quo.

I interviewed the three original Anagrammists in February 2007 shortly before the theatrical release of *Fido*. *Fido* is a satire of zombie films set in Willard, a small town lost in the idyllic world of the 1950s, where the sun shines every day, everybody knows their neighbour, and zombies carry the mail. "Canadian director Andrew Currie has crafted a smart and funny genre mash-up—it's a boy and his dog picture in which the dog is a ravenous if good-natured zombie. The tone is pure fifties melodrama, with a script leavened by black comedy and satire" (*Globe and Mail*).

Andrew Currie. Photo by Clancy Dennehy.

Andrew Currie (*b.* 1962) is an intense young man with a passion for film, and Canadian film in particular. We met in Anagram's home office, a large warren of offices near Vancouver's Commercial Drive. All of Andrew's films, including his acclaimed short film *Night of the Living*, and the features *Mile Zero* and *Fido* are about the inability of fathers and sons to communicate with each other.

Thompson When and where did you start making films?
Currie I studied at Simon Fraser University from 1989 to 1993 and that's where I met Trent Carlson. We hit it off right away. We're like-minded about filmmaking. That's also where I met Bob Aschmann [the director of photography on *Mile Zero*]. Trent, Bob, and I worked on each other's projects. We have a great shared work ethic and belief in collaboration. We'd often be "up on the hill" at sfu editing at 4 a.m.

I loved SFU — it was film history and film theory, and it really built a foundation for me as an artist and filmmaker and set a course for the kind of filmmaker I want to be.

SFU was experimental. Chris Welsby [a renowned experimental film-maker] was my first-year teacher and a huge inspiration. I had no real belief in my own artistic abilities and I had a lot of strange ideas. I remember sitting down with Chris and unloading this really weird idea for a movie and him saying, "That's great, what else do you have?" He embraced the idea of expressing yourself regardless of what the idea was. I'd always felt pushed into boxes and Chris was the opposite of that. I loved SFU—it was film history and film theory, and it really built a foundation for me as an artist and filmmaker and set a course for the kind of filmmaker I want to be.

Thompson How did you and Trent form Anagram?

Currie Trent and I were making short films at the time. Truthfully, shorts are as hard as making features, and some people don't realize that. The process of making the film is the same, so we both made conscious decisions to start writing features, which is what we did, and formed a

The critiques at the Film Centre were painfully honest and that's where I learned to have a tougher skin. Dezso would say, "There are no clothes on in this room."

writers' group and focused on understanding narrative structure in a feature form.

Trent and I formed Anagram in 1996—we made Trent's short film *Groomed*, which we co-edited and co-produced. And as soon as it was finished editing I was accepted into the Canadian Film Centre and left Vancouver in the summer of 1996.

Thompson And that's where you made *Night of the Living*, about a boy whose father becomes a zombie when he drinks?

Currie Yes. The Film Centre was a great place for me to be. I met a lot of writers and directors whom I admire. The director Dezso Magyar was inspiring and, unlike SFU, his focus was character and story. He put a huge emphasis on that. He mentored with István Szabó, the director of *Mephisto*, and he had a strong European sensibility.

The Film Centre is great. You're either writing, in prep, shooting, in post, or critiquing. No breaks. No rest. I did about six short projects,

Opposite: Andrew Currie directs Michael Riley as Derek in *Mile Zero*. *Above*: Currie directing Michael Riley and Connor Widdows. Both photos by Carol Racicot.

most of them scene studies. The critiques were painfully honest and that's where I learned to have a tougher skin. Dezso would say, "There are no clothes on in this room." It was hard on people but it made you grow quickly.

Thompson *Night of the Living* is a wonderful film, which played festivals world-wide including Sundance, and it won several short film awards including the Telefilm award for Best New Director at the Vancouver Film Festival. Would you describe it for me?

Currie My films are always about parents. I think that comes from my own fears about not being a good parent—and I love zombies. They're a metaphoric sponge, the multi-purpose metaphor. I was watching zombie movies and was interested in addiction at the time, particularly alcoholism and how prevalent it was. And there was this perfect metaphor for brain damage. It was great to tell it from the point of view of a child. The story is about a boy whose father turns into a zombie when he drinks, although the boy is the only one who sees it. The boy's afraid of his father because he's a zombie, but of course he also loves him.

Thompson *Mile Zero* is also about fear of the parent.

Currie I know. The genesis of *Mile Zero* came when I was at the Film Centre. I was only seeing my two-year-old son in Vancouver every four or five weeks. It made me feel like a bad parent. That was difficult. *Mile Zero* became an expression of that space. I also wanted to explore male vulnerability. I hadn't seen it expressed that often in movies and it was certainly something I was feeling and I needed to explore.

The father Derek [Michael Riley] has a lot of fear. The way a lot of men express vulnerability is through anger and aggression. I have male friends who hold onto a lot of their anger, and it's a problem. There isn't really a platform for men to be truly vulnerable. I find it sad that we're a culture that's like that. I've travelled a lot to different festivals and in Spanish-language cultures, where men are more comfortable with being open and vulnerable and emotional. Our lack of openness is conditioned. At least I hope we're not born this way.

Thompson *Fido*, your next film, seems to build perfectly from *Night of the Living* and *Mile Zero*.

Currie *Fido* is about a boy who prefers a zombie to his father. It wasn't a conscious development, from *Night of the Living* to *Mile Zero* to *Fido*, even though you look back and see such an obvious path.

Thompson You co-wrote the screenplay.

Currie Yes, and that was a long process. In 1994 Dennis Heaton, Robert Chomiak, and I were close friends and wanted to write a project together. We had everyone bring five ideas to the table, and Dennis had

My films are always about parents. I think that comes from my own fears about not being a good parent—and I love zombies.

Opposite: Still from *Fido*. Bill (Dylan Baker), Fido (Billy Connolly), Timmy (K'Sun Ray), and Helen (Carrie-Anne Moss) at the cemetery. Photo by Michael Courtney.

written a story about a boy and his pet zombie. The boy stopped his pet from eating people by giving it raw meat, and so we fleshed out that idea and made it *Fido*.

Once we finished I took it out to the Film Centre and it was optioned by a company out there. And then it got trapped in three years of an option phase. And then about 2003 Anagram optioned it back. And that's when it came back into the story room here. It was post 9/11 and there was this sense that the film could express something about homeland security and the state of the world and still maintain its place as a comedy and a satire. The premise is that years ago, the earth passed through a cloud of space dust, causing the dead to rise with an insatiable hunger for human flesh. Terror spreads across the land, until a collar is invented that makes the zombies docile. And so the zombies become gardeners, milkmen, servants, even pets. Hence, Fido, the zombie.

> It was post 9/11 and there was this sense that the film could express something about homeland security and the state of the world and still maintain its place as a comedy and a satire.

Thompson Tell me about the Anagram story room.

Currie The story room has always been an incredibly positive experience. We approach all our stories from the point of view of character and theme. For *Fido* we defined the theme as "love, not fear, makes us more alive." Bill the father is afraid of zombies, but also of human intimacy and love. But Fido the zombie is more emotionally alive than Bill. Bill's demise and Fido's integration into the family as father and partner is the backbone of the story. At the San Francisco Independent Film Festival they talked about "Fido" as a metaphor for alternate lifestyles.

Thompson What's the trick to making the extraordinary seem real and believable?

Currie The most pleasurable part of making the film but also the most challenging was setting the tone. For me the key was keeping the performances real. I didn't want the actors performing with a nudge and a wink. They had to believe the world that they were in. I call it "repressed camp."

At SFU I was terrible with actors and couldn't understand them. It became my obsession and focus. I learned to work out what's motivating them beat by beat through the whole film. I remember watching

I didn't want the actors performing with a nudge and a wink. They had to believe the world that they were in. I call it "repressed camp."

Still from *Fido*. Helen (Carrie-Anne Moss) dances with Fido (Billy Connolly). Photo by Michael Courtney.

one student film and the filmmaker had cut off everyone's heads (in the framing). The filmmaker said, "I'm showing how marginalized these characters are." It was ridiculous. But in a funny way it helped me realize how elements in a film need to be integrated in a way that people can connect to or understand. Otherwise, who are you making it for? If it's just for yourself you're not doing the film any service.

Thompson *Fido* is both stylish and stylized. Can you talk about that?

Currie The art direction in *Fido* is critical to the film. Fairly early on in the process of writing I saw the film in a Technicolor wide-screen way. Probably the best thing I did was to make paintings of key images in my head. I also worked with Ricardo Sandoval, and I found black-and-white images from the '40s and '50s—images like a guy pumping gas—and in Photoshop we turned him into a zombie. That helped people with the tone. We also used clips from *All That Heaven Allows*. That helped a lot. With the music, I started working with Don MacDonald a year before. Don's a brilliant composer and he's done *Kissed* and the Bruce Sweeney films. So *Fido* was the perfect movie for him. He's a classically trained violinist in an orchestra, and he's conducted orchestras. *Fido* has this big '50s orchestral score. I put all those elements onto a DVD, what we call a style book, and sent that out with the script. It really helped.

Thompson What's next for you?

Currie I'm writing "The Truth about Lying" formerly known as "Sperm." It's about a guy in his late twenties. He's a sort of a Walter Mitty type who's paralyzed by expectations from his mother. His father died when he was one, so all he knows is what his mother's told him and what he's seen in home videos. His father was a fighter pilot, orchestra conductor, brain surgeon. Well. It turns out those were all lies. His mother went to a sperm bank and then created this fiction about the father. It's about a family of liars.

Thompson What are your feelings about Canadian film these days?

Currie I'm really excited about Canadian film. I grew up on Atom Egoyan, David Cronenberg, and Patricia Rozema, and I love Canadian film.

The art direction in *Fido* is critical to the film.... Probably the best thing I did was to make paintings of key images in my head. I found black-and-white images from the '40s and '50s—images like a guy pumping gas—and in Photoshop we turned him into a zombie.

What's sad is this desire to place Canadian filmmakers in commercial boxes or art house boxes. I feel that if you look at a lot of the great indie filmmakers they manage to entertain and make meaningful films. The key is originality. The funniest people in the world are Canadian. I think about Australia in the '90s and films like *Muriel's Wedding* and *Proof* that could not have come out of anywhere but Oz, and Canada can do that too. We can't be Hollywood. Our US distributor Lionsgate said only a Canadian could have written *Fido!* So they know something about us that I'm not sure even we know.

My next interview was with **Trent Carlson**, a deceptively low-key talker who has an incisive mind and a great sense of humour. His award-winning short films—which have played festivals worldwide, including Sundance—include *Groomed*, *Around the Corner*, and *The Station*.

Thompson How did you get started?

Carlson When I saw Anne Wheeler's film *Bye-Bye Blues*, I thought you can actually do this in Canada. I was driving a truck in Alberta, and I realized for the first time you can be a filmmaker in Canada. I came out to Vancouver to study at Simon Fraser University.

Thompson Why do you think you and Andrew hooked up?

Carlson We share a huge love for story and felt and still feel that the script is everything. We committed at Simon Fraser University to working together. Our first step was to form writing groups and learn how to write.

Trent Carlson. Photo by Clancy Dennehy.

During that time we continued to work together and write together, and we remained committed to keeping control of our stories. We made short films but we weren't meeting any producers. Then we met Blake Corbet. Blake and I are both from Alberta, and we started sharing info. Blake was going through a transition from directing stage plays to short films. He also had his own construction company. Andrew and I felt we didn't have the business sense to build a larger company. Blake was a good fit. We started to meet regularly and although Blake was contemplating a move to Toronto, we talked him into staying and joining us. The three of us committed to making the feature films *Mile Zero* and *The Delicate Art of Parking* to test drive the relationship. Blake and I were the producers on *Mile Zero* and Andrew was the writer/director. Ask Blake about losing the distributor four days before the shoot. It was one of those "the sky is falling" moments. It was a huge learning process for all of us, facing the realties of what we knew and what we didn't know. And looking at how we as a group could continue to grow and work together.

Ask Blake about losing the distributor four days before the shoot. It was one of those "the sky is falling" moments.

Thompson How did *The Delicate Art of Parking* come about?

Carlson The idea for the story came out of real-life experience. I had parked illegally, ran into a store, and returned a few minutes later only to find a guy placing a parking ticket on my windshield. I unloaded on

With *The Delicate Art of Parking* it was a real-life experience that inspired a personal exploration into the meaning of work.

him and then immediately regretted it. I'm a calm guy by nature, so got the feeling if I'm doing this, a lot of people have to be. I started thinking what it would be like to get yelled at all day long on a regular basis and thought there might be a great opportunity to create an interesting comedic anti-hero. I brought a first draft into our story room and ended up collaborating with my partner Blake on the script. We shot the final script, but I also did a lot of improv with the performers during shooting so I think a good portion of the writing credit has to go to the actors. With *The Delicate Art of Parking* it was a real-life experience that inspired a personal exploration into the meaning of work.

Thompson *Parking* won best Canadian film at the Montreal World Film Festival. Tell me about the Montreal connection.

Carlson We released *The Delicate Art of Parking* with a Montreal company called Cinema Libre, a wonderful company, sadly no longer in business. This was the largest film they'd been involved with and the first in English.

Opposite: Trent Carlson directs Fred Ewanuick on the set of *The Delicate Art of Parking*. Photo by Murray Forward. *Above*: An angry car owner returns to his car to find that Grant (Fred Ewanuick) has written him a ticket. Photo by Bob Akester.

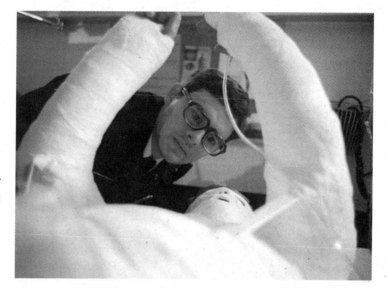

There are advantages to being in the West. We're a smaller community and you know more about what everyone else is doing, especially here in Vancouver.

Still from the *Delicate Art of Parking*. Grant (Fred Ewanuick) tends to his best friend and mentor, Murray Schwartz, in the hospital. Photo by Bob Akester.

Releasing a film is hard. As a filmmaker, I think you need to be there on the opening weekend, when people show up or don't show up. Movies cost a lot of money to make and to release. It's fiercely competitive to get your film into the theatre for the first weekend. We have big respect for the distributor. The film was out there in the Canadian *Zeitgeist* and enough people had heard it about and seen it. It did very well at the Canadian box office, but the film hasn't travelled as much internationally as I would have liked.

I've played it at enough festivals down in the US to know that they get it. Car culture is everywhere. But the film didn't get big exposure. Distributors looked at it and said, "It's a little too much work for us, there's no star." It's starting to make international sales now.

Thompson Would you say Canadian film is healthy at the moment?

Carlson I can only talk about Western Canadian film. I think there are advantages to being in the West. We're a smaller community and you know more about what everyone else is doing, especially here in Vancouver. It's kind of the centre of the western universe as opposed to the eastern universe in Toronto. It's the same kind of frustration if you're an Albertan, or from Saskatchewan, because things are run out of Vancouver. A lot of the people you need to talk with are centred here. Telefilm, Movie Central, BC Film are people we can see, go for coffee with.

I don't think any of us have felt we can't make the movies we want to make because we're not in Toronto. But of course we want to cross borders and become more international. I know there's always more media attention and hype around filmmakers based in Toronto and that's fine. I don't feel any animosity about that. None of that changes your movie so if you're reacting to that, well, it's more about ego. And that's not why I'm making movies. I'm more interested in telling the story and connecting with people.

The next phase for us is discovering how our stories can be truly universal. How can we cast that will help? How can we establish relationships with US distributors, international sales agents, executive producers so that you can get that perspective about what your story can use in order to widen its appeal? Sometimes people acquaint making it more commercial with making it less unique, but that's not true. I believe there's a hunger for film that's riskier, unique, and uniquely Canadian. With some smart choices you can open it up in ways that are rewarding for you and for your audiences locally and globally.

Blake Corbet. Photo by Clancy Dennehy.

Blake Corbet (*b*. 1961) is a dynamic director, producer, and writer. His films as a director include *The Chain*, starring Molly Parker. He co-wrote *The Delicate Art of Parking*, was producer on *Mile Zero*, *The Delicate Art of Parking*, and *Fido*, and was co-producer on the Danny Glover film *Missing in America*.

Thompson Tell me how you became involved with Anagram and about the philosophy behind the group.

Corbet I joined eight years ago. We're looking at films with some social conscience; we're driven to make films with important themes. You can have a message built into a film that isn't a "message film," and our films do that.

Thompson Can you elaborate on the role of a producer?

Corbet I liken a producer to a developer. A real estate developer sees a piece of land, wants to buy it, and then hires an architect to design however many units you want to put on the land. The developer decides who the units are going to be for, empty nesters or first-time buyers. Then you raise the money. You own the property. You hire everybody and ultimately reap the benefits if it's successful. And that's what a producer does. You look for properties to develop. A lot of the time producers in Canada are running dogs of the directors. They find a producer to do the work for them.

Thompson Tell me about your own film background.

Corbet I made my first short film in 1982 when I was an English major at Carleton University. They had a big journalism school there and they also had a lot of old film cameras. I was taking a film studies class and you could make a film rather than write an essay and I got the bug. I'd been taking Creative Writing and wanted to be a writer but when I realized how much fun making movies was, that was that. I learned about photography and framing and reframing in the darkroom. I learned about grain and contrasts. So I learned a lot about photography and writing and actors. Ever since, I've wanted to be a filmmaker. It's been a long route, though.

I went to Simon Fraser University in 1985–86. Somewhere there's an SFU film I never finished. I never liked the rushes. I still have trouble with rushes. Rushes make me want to throw myself off a bridge. I find them so intensely disappointing. I have a lot of trouble with the post process, but my partners help me through that.

Thompson You and Trent produced Andrew's first feature *Mile Zero*. Tell me about that.

Corbet Shortly after film school I made *The Chain*, got married, and

> You can have a message built into a film that isn't a "message film," and our films do that.

SC: 28   SHT: 11
A ZOMBIE (FIDO) LUMBERS ,,
CARRYING A ROAST ON A
PLATTER.

SC: 28   SHT: 12
O/ TIMMY;

HELEN:
" ISN'T HE WONDERFUL ? "

SC: 28   SHT: 13
HELEN (CONT):
" NOW WE'RE NOT THE
ONLY ONES... "
THE ZOMBIE MOVES.
WE PAN...

ZOMBIE !!!

PAN

CONT.

SC: 28   SHT: 13A
··· RIGHT AS THE ZOMBIE-

HELEN (CONT):
··· ON THE STREET WITH
ONE."
··· STEPS UP TO BILL.
BILL RECOILS. HE DROPS
HIS MARTINI.

PAN

SC: 28   SHT: 14

SMASH!

THE MARTINI HITS THE
GROUND.

(3)   / /

Rushes make me want to
throw myself off a bridge.
I have a lot of trouble with
the post process, but my
partners help me through.

Storyboard for *Fido*.
Storyboard art by Rob Pratt.

had three kids. It was hard to become a full-time filmmaker. I had a construction company. I'd pave driveways and do landscaping. I needed that to keep the family going.

I dabbled in film and dabbled in theatre, which I loved because it has no post-production process. You get the play just how you like it and you learn about blocking, performance, staging, set decorating, lighting, and costumes. There's everything you need to make a film except a camera. Blocking for the stage is different but it's still blocking. I built my company up to the point where I could sell it. I sold it in 1998. I was looking for a team because I saw companies grow more quickly when there was a team involved. It was a gestalt thing. I had a lot of business skills, and then Trent and Andrew asked me to come on board for *Mile Zero* and *The Delicate Art of Parking*. I ended up writing on those scripts and learning about the Canadian financing system.

There's nothing easy in this business.

There's nothing easy in this business. I went to an indie film financing conference in San Francisco a few years back called IFFCON and met a group of US producers who were also trying to raise money. We were trying to do *Mile Zero* and were pretty hopeful we could get Telefilm and BC Film on board. The US producers felt I had it easy, being able to access those public sources of funding when everything they have to raise has to come from the studios or private money. As a result, Americans think a lot more about the development process. If they don't get an audience, they're sunk. Granted, many young producers are rich kids who might have a safety net, but it's not as difficult here as it is south of the border.

Thompson What is your philosophy as a producer?

Corbet To me, again, script development is like land development. Your goal is to get the greatest value added. If you've got an idea for a piece of property, where you add the value is in the zoning. I've learned to carefully choose what property to develop. Your film is still going to be summarized in one sentence—for the sales agent, for the audience—and that's something that's never going to change. You ask yourself what's the reward, financially and artistically, in your life?

We look at a lot of projects and ideas, and, ultimately, being able to see what it is clearly is the first and most important thing. You have to get excited about it and then see what it is, and make it into a story that will be compelling.

Thompson *Fido* had a large budget. Can you talk about that?

Corbet *Fido* was pretty scary. We believed we could do it and we were able to convince a couple of executives at Telefilm we could do it. We had the huge advantage of the Canadian system. When you're in Los Angeles and you can say I can bring $5 million into the project that's a huge leg up. It makes it easier for the numbers to work for the people you're going after. We were able to get Lionsgate because it made it easier for them to work with us.

The film had a lot of challenges. We started to deal with some cast that were very sought after and their reps. We hadn't cast from the Hollywood system. These actors have a lot of representation. That was all brand new for us. We were dealing with fifteen different lawyers, eleven sources of money. I'd have conference calls with five different lawyers.

Everybody wanted *Fido* to happen and, as hard it was, I think it can be a lot harder. When you're making a film with an interesting theme, people go easier on you. When you're into those phone calls, people know that what you're doing isn't strictly business. They're all defending their clients but the overall goal becomes to get this done.

Thompson What was your role in the actual making of the film?

Corbet I was involved in all the key creative aspects, which include production design, hiring the first assistant director, the composer, the director of photography, the editor, and all the casting, particularly the leads but all the way down to anyone with a speaking part. I was involved in the costume design and approving all those elements, and after that I didn't have a lot to do. Well, there were script changes. There were script changes right up to the end with Carrie-Anne Moss because we had to write her pregnancy into the story.

Then there's closing the financing. There's a date on which the company that bonds the film sends an e-mail to the banker and then the

> We were dealing with fifteen different lawyers, eleven sources of money. I'd have conference calls with five different lawyers.

banker sends a fax to release the money. We'd already spent a million but there was $9.7 million I couldn't touch, and that came through the day before we started principal photography. I closed at 12:30 in the afternoon and walked down the hall for a cast read-through, and then Mary Anne Waterhouse took over and ran the film.

Thompson What advice do you have for young filmmakers?

Corbet For years Canadians seemed to shy away from genre pictures, but that's changing, now, and you can say a lot within a genre.

Thompson How do you see this time in Canadian film?

Corbet Telefilm doubled the amount of money they invest four or five years ago. The Canadian Television Fund is still standing. Everybody asks why hasn't Canadian film broken through? But in terms of the US, those of us who make films for under $10 million are the little guys. And for every *Blair Witch* there're a couple of thousand guys sleeping under bridges.

■

For every *Blair Witch* there're a couple of thousand guys sleeping under bridges.

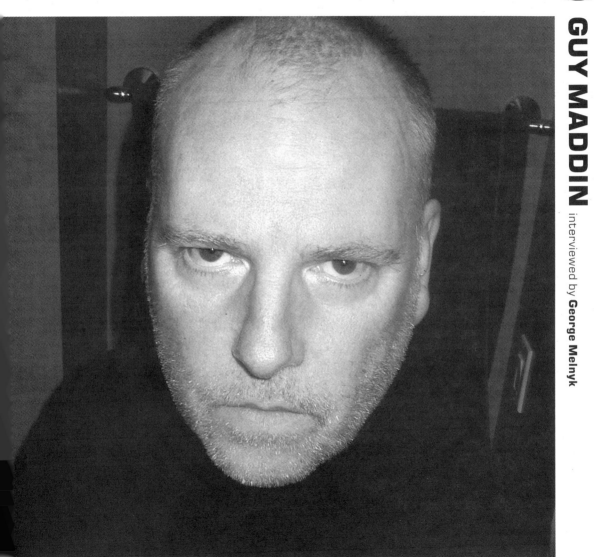

GUY MADDIN

interviewed by **George Melnyk**

SELF-PORTRAIT, SEPTEMBER 2007

Melnyk You've been a filmmaker who started in Winnipeg and continued doing your filmmaking there. What does it mean to you to be called a Winnipeg filmmaker?

Maddin I just turned fifty this past winter [2006] and by coincidence I was working on a documentary on Winnipeg for the Documentary Channel, which had invited filmmakers to do autobiographical, deeply personal portraits of their hometowns. I was encouraged to eschew objectivity and make the documentary about my *own* Winnipeg, and definitely not a travelogue. I really started thinking a lot about my relationship with the city and eventually I ended up brooding. I took the dog for long walks. We both, the dog and I, managed to avoid freezing just by daydreaming, thinking about I'm not sure what, but I got reflecting on the real atrocities of time's passage. The city was founded in 1874.

Because my mother was old when I was born and her mother was old when she was born, I had a grandmother who was born the same year the city was and I knew her until I was fourteen, when she died. It is hard to believe Winnipeg came to be during the lifetime of someone I knew. I always thought of this city as so ancient, its buildings mythically crammed with too many lives to account for, and then I realized it's only two or three generations old. It really did a mind mess on me, and I started thinking about how quickly my own life is going by. It just made me feel pretty insignificant; made me kind of claustrophobic; made me feel like maybe I should get out of here before I'm stuck in the lockstep of the city, before I squander my time on earth simply by not leaving. I spent the first half century of my life daydreaming of what the city could be like in the future and now I realize I'll never live long enough to see the city become those things. And it won't ever become those things anyway. Even if my wildest daydreams came true, it could never become the wonderful *place* I wanted it to be. Maybe I should reread *Portrait of the Artist as a Young Man*. All I remember about that book is some young man feeling a lot of discomfort with who he was, with his hometown, his homeland even, *until he leaves*. I'm beginning to won-

> I always thought of this city as so ancient, and then I realized it's only two or three generations old. It really did a mind mess on me, and I started thinking about how quickly my own life is going by.

der if by the time we edit that documentary I'll be kissing this place goodbye.

Melnyk Do you think it's some kind of a mid-career or a mid-life crisis you're talking about?

Maddin What I've heard is that mid-life crisis hits you in an area of strength. It doesn't get you where you expect it to hurt, in your areas of weakness, for instance. It'll get you in the areas you feel most certain about. I guess that's what's getting to me right now. Time's *once-sweet* passage, my comfort within the buildings, avenues, and memories that have *always* meant so much to me—everything's gone flavourless. It feels like I've used those memories too much, that I've sucked the flavour out of them and I can't reconstitute any of it. Maybe it is some kind of crisis after all.

I have a few friends here in Winnipeg who always recharge me, leave me excited, tickled, and mischievous, ready to roll. When I'm in Toronto,

> What I've heard is that mid-life crisis hits you in an area of strength.

Guy Maddin, with Super 8 camera, shooting *Dracula: Pages from a Virgin's Diary*, September 2001. Photo by deco dawson.

The Village Voice once described me as either the most accessible experimental filmmaker or the most experimental mainstream filmmaker working today.

not so much. George Toles, my longtime collaborator, is still big for me, and I have Noam Gonick, Nihad Ademi, Evan Johnson, John Harvie, and some other friends in town who get me excited. But I'm weary because parasitically sucking inspiration from others is the system I've used for twenty years now, and I'm scared to change it. But people, once sucked almost dry, are aware that change is necessary.

Melnyk Winnipeg is a strange place when I think about your films. Winnipeg these days is considered parochial, small, mid-western, and yet there's all this cosmopolitan imagination that keeps bubbling up from the gumbo. *The Saddest Music in the World* is both global and local.

Maddin I would like to position myself in the centre of things. Winnipeg is in fact located at the geographic centre of North America. And as if to rhyme that factoid, Jim Hoberman of *The Village Voice* once described me as either the most accessible experimental filmmaker or the most experimental mainstream filmmaker working today, something centrist.

I've always thought of myself, in my most private moments, as an artist—a painter, let's say—and I have a little palette with all the little paints at my disposal.

I'm proud of that description, but I never forget what's at the centre of donuts, our civic comestible.

Melnyk If you take the adjective "experimental" and the adjective "cult," you know they're really both completely opposite sides. Cult films can have an audience of millions, right? And experimental films can have an audience of three. I don't think you're either. So maybe just the film critic is right about you walking this line somewhere in the middle of experimental and cult.

Maddin I like so many different kinds of films and I ... I've always thought of myself, in my most private moments, as an artist—a painter, let's say—and I have a little palette with all the little paints at my disposal. There's silent movie mime, naturalistic acting, Sensurround, 3D, Odorama, etc. I can choose from among them to paint right on the movie screen. I can apply any one of them I want in the hope I'll somehow make them work together. Every filmmaker has that option, too. Why

Opposite: Louis Negin as Dr. Fusi, the craven abortionist in *Cowards Bend the Knee*, 2002. *Above*: Darcy Fehr as Guy Maddin and Amy Stewart as Veronica in *Cowards Bend the Knee*. Both photos by Guy Maddin.

⑦ Dark, Foggy
Belly moves ever so slightly
Selznick talking

⑧
IR swings head in reaction to Fellini's Voice
Fellini talking

⑨ From Out of thick Fog
Fellini strides down aisle between ruined seats

②

⑩
C.U. Fellini finishing his line, stopping at the footlights

⑲
UP IN THE LOGE, THE SILHOUETTE OF HITCHCOCK. FINISHING HIS LONG WHEEZING INTAKE OF AIR BEFORE SPEAKING. THEN: "Bloody right... etc."

⑳ Rear Screen
I.R. joins Fellini to listen, both entranced, both staring up at the loge and Hitchcock.

20A

20A
Selznick turns away back to reading his book

㉑
Chaplin jauntily walks on stage, emerges from fog on stage left, looks up at shadow in loge, tips cap.

⑪
Belly listens awhile impassively

⑫
Fellini finishes

⑬ ⑭ ⑮
C.U.'s CUT AMONG BELLY, FELLINI & ISABELLA (LISTENING)
BELLY JIGGLING ANGRILY ON "WET DREAMS."

㉒
Selznick sits up to watch Chaplin.

㉓ (Rear Screen
IR + Fellini stare at Chaplin with awe and love.

⑯ REAR SCREEN
I.R. & SELZNICK THEIR EYES, AS IF WATCHING TENNIS, LISTENING BACK AND FORTH

⑰
CN. Fellini frustrated by RR.'s argument
HEARS WHEEZE & looks up to loge suddenly

⑱ REAR SCREEN
I.R. & SELZNICK CRANE NECKS UP TO LOGE Toward wheeze

㉔ CHAPLIN APPROACHES BELLY
BELLY IN FOREGROUND

㉕
CHAPLIN SPEAKS

Above and opposite: Guy Maddins's storyboards for *My Dad Is 100 Years Old.*

should I put these paints on in any way other than what I feel is best? Painters don't worry about that, so why should I?

Melnyk Your interest in the melodramatic style of the silent film seems profound. These were popular mainstream films in their day but seem archaic to us today. And yet you have found an audience for your resurrection of this style.

Maddin I was just reading an interview with David Lynch that he did with film reviewer John Powers in 1986, and he was talking about how in 1986 movies had to be cruel and they had to be unemotional to be cruel, because people were too worried about expressing themselves emotion-

DEBATE OF THE IMMORTALS
THERE IS A SENSE THAT THE BELLY IS IN BED, ON THE STAGE

98

I.R: "What about the great Anna Magnani?"

99

100 I.B.
Belly says back

"She was different."

THE LIGHTNING BOLT STRIKES AT THE ANGRY GRAB O' THE GENITALS

MORE COSMIC MURK

ALL THE CARPING & DISSENTING DISEMBODIED VOICES

ISABELLA IN A THICK FOG, TRYING TO MAKE OUT THE SOURCE OF THESE VOICES

3A WIDER (IN FOG)

SHE STANDS AMONG THE SEATS OF THE BROKEN-DOWN THEATRE

101
Wolf shadow appears, small and far back in the theatre

102 Rear screen
Selznick & Fellini look over shoulders to source of growling.

102 From behind screen
I.R. also looking back toward growls, she returns gaze to her mother

104 I.R. "Was Anna hurt...?"
SAME as 98

102 A
Hitch strains famous profile to listen to growls.

Fog clears to reveal D.O. Selznick sitting in a theatre seat, or backwards on a seat back. A stack of books by his side, a book in hand, stogie in lips. He starts to speak. "Film is art..."

c.u. SELZNICK (CONTINUES TO SPEAK) "It comes from storytelling."

c.u. I.R.'s eyes check out RR's belly to see how her father is taking in all this Selznick talk. Her eyes dart between the sitting producer and her father, in bed and on stage.

ally and unironically. Then Powers asked Lynch what people worried about in the 1950s and he said radiation. He said that the radiation had become an emotion. I think what Lynch said twenty years ago stands now, that people are embarrassed by melodrama, an unironic expression of our innermost fears. Which is what melodrama is, right, it's just a magic glass put on our foreheads to help us see what worries us in our dreams. Not a magnifying glass but some kind of special viewing glass. In good melodrama, you don't have to worry about whether style or content *is* hip or not. We think the same way now as humans did during the time of Euripides. Probably the same way we did when we were making melodramatic cave paintings with berry juice 50,000 years before that. That's

Melodrama is a magic glass put on our foreheads to help us see what worries us in our dreams.

I give to myself the assignment of making bigger-than-life, completely uninhibited, and therefore honest, portraits of real psychologically plausible people.

Guy Maddin peers into his self-designed matte box on the set of *Careful*, 1991. Photo by Jeff Solylo.

what's reassuring, exciting, and exhilarating when you read Euripides. He reads like a comic book, really crazy, wild, and fearless. Not afraid to be tasteless or too big, and that's exciting to me. I give to myself the assignment of making bigger-than-life, completely uninhibited, and therefore honest, portraits of real psychologically plausible people. It's a hard thing to do, but if I ever get it right I shall have made a good melodrama.

Melnyk Any thoughts on the documentary that Noam Gonick made about you? It dealt with the making of *Twilight of the Ice Nymphs*.

Maddin I haven't seen it yet. Noam is a good friend and we had a deal ten years ago when he made the thing that I wouldn't watch it. I can't. I just couldn't. It's sheer vanity and terror. I don't want to see or hear myself. Unhealthy of me, I know, but that's all there is to it.

Ice Nymphs didn't have a good vibe for me. On earlier projects I'd always been able to cast a spell around myself. I probably say this in the documentary, but while working on that movie I couldn't get myself into a trance. I couldn't go into that little dreamy spell where I believed what I was making mattered to me. And I didn't like working with the producer I had. He was assigned to me—an unfortunate arranged marriage. I don't think I ever got inside the script properly; I really let it down. Not having been there on the inside of the beginning I don't think I ever understood it as thoroughly as I did the stories George [Toles] and I had previously worked on from their very beginnings. So I kind of did this half-assed service to the script and then ultimately I got lazy and gave up. I've been fighting laziness my whole life. I just fell back into it and let the movie direct itself. Movies will direct themselves, you know.

Melnyk So let me ask about your obsession with making shorts.

Maddin I never had an obsession with shorts before but now I do. They're so easy to do, not so easy to do well, but at least they don't take so long. You just get a little idea and it's over very quickly. In the process of gathering together collaborators to shoot this little thing, you've staved off loneliness and doubts about your ability to aim a camera. You just kept the rust off your eyeballs. Shooting shorts has really turned into something I like.

Melnyk And you don't have to raise half a million bucks at a time, right?

Maddin No, later I'll show you the two-minute short we made in two hours. It just might be the stupidest, most pointless thing we've ever made. It's called *The Nude Caboose*. My producer Jody Shapiro and I shot it with cell phones. It was my very first cell phone movie—the first of many I hope. It's dumb but it felt good.

Melnyk Do you ever go back to see your shorts?

Maddin Yeah, every now and then. Some of them I like. And some of them are terrible, and I've even started to remove their titles from my filmography. I don't make them available. And some of them would cost too much money to make available. They were edited to uncleared

> I never had an obsession with shorts before but now I do. They're so easy to do, not so easy to do well, but at least they don't take so long.

I knew right from the beginning that I'd be a primitive filmmaker because I was coming very late to everything technical.

Above: Leslie Bais as Anna the State Scientist in *The Heart of the World*, 2000. Photo by deco dawson. *Opposite*: Maya Lawson as Sis and Sullivan Brown as Guy Maddin in *Brand upon the Brain!*, 2006. Photo by Adam I. Weintraub.

music. I don't circulate those now that I have a bit of a profile. Some of them I enjoy; I'll proudly pop on "Heart of the World." It somehow turned out exactly the way I envisioned it and that never happens with features.

Melnyk You are quite a literary person. You write reviews for *The Village Voice* and have published several books.

Maddin I like the visuals that great writing gives to you—a really intoxicating view that only a metaphor can offer. When I started making movies, I knew right from the beginning that I'd be a primitive filmmaker because I was coming very late to everything technical, that if I studied for twenty years I'd never be able to catch up with technology. So what I tried to do right from the start was to resist temptations to polish the films, but rather strive to create through the writing the same heavenly thrill one gets reading a metaphor that takes you a lot further than you expect it to. I tried to create that same feeling with my film writing, writing done with the camera. I don't think I ever succeeded, but this grand attempt was what got me started.

Melnyk In an interview that you did that I picked up on the Net, you talked about how you'd like to live for a long time in the Russian film archives. I can imagine you in Moscow. But it wouldn't have to be in today's Russia. It would have to be in a black-and-white kind of Stalinist Russia or a communist Russia where everything was black and white.

Maddin The siege of the Moscow film archives!

Melnyk Let's say you'd been born in the Soviet Union in 1919 or 1950. And you'd become a filmmaker. What kind of filmmaker do you imagine you would've become?

Maddin I don't know, probably one quickly stuck in a gulag somewhere. But the idea of going backwards to find the future is really exhilarating to me. I've been invited to go to a number of events in Russia. At one point I was just scared to because someone had kept me up all night telling me Russian mafia horror stories and I just cancelled my flight. I'd go if

> The idea of going backwards to find the future is really exhilarating to me.

I was invited again. I'd go to north-end Winnipeg and buy a pair of felt boots for the trip.

Melnyk I want to ask you about economics. You got a degree in economics. So what is your assessment of the economics of your career?

Maddin Economically speaking, my films have been a disaster because they don't make much money for anybody. I get a salary off some of them. You can live pretty comfortably here for reasonable sums. I live in a mansion in Winnipeg and all I pay is a thousand dollars a month for rent. I guess I'm happy right now because I'm still able to make movies. Although I have noticed the budgets for my movies have gone down instead of up. That isn't because I failed to secure bigger budgets. I haven't even tried. I made *The Saddest Music in the World* for $3.5 million. That was my most expensive movie, made three years ago. Since then I haven't even tried to raise that kind of money.

Melnyk How much money has it made back?

Maddin I think it did okay for its distributor, but I'm not sure.

Melnyk One of the things I wanted to talk about is the subconscious. What's your own assessment of the role of the subconscious in your films?

Maddin I've read a bit of Freud, but I found he actually ruined dreams for me. I caught myself trying to analyze the dreams while I was having them. And so it took me about a year to enjoy dreaming again. I have this approach to people, this model of how people think, mostly based on my own reading and movie experiences, as well as some actual contact with living people, that I apply like a boilerplate to familiar situations to see if I understand what's happening or not. Every now and then I recognize someone I know from books in the secret wishes of someone I know in real life. I'll see in a friend going through a bad divorce the character of Medea, who kills her children just to hurt the husband who left her. I like to file away the feeling of satisfaction enjoyed when a real person metamorphoses into someone on the page and then back into someone I know again. I just try to work the same subconscious mechanisms, recognize and plagiarize the great myths, keep copying, just as people have always copied literature and literature people, always.

> I just try to work the same subconscious mechanisms, recognize and plagiarize the great myths, keep copying, just as people have copied literature and literature people, always.

I'm horrified to discover that I'm fifty, because I really do feel that I'm still working on some pretty juvenile emotions, which I'm just starting to understand.

Melnyk Now I want to go a little bit back into the past. Do you ever sit back and ask yourself what brought you to where you are at fifty?

Maddin I'm shockingly unchanged since I picked up a camera. In a way that's enabled me to keep going. I haven't learned that much but I'm still trying to do the same thing, the same simple thing. After 2000 I just unlearned how to play all my instruments and I became a garage band again and I feel a lot happier about it. I'm horrified to discover that I'm fifty, because I really do feel that I'm still working on some pretty juvenile emotions, which I'm just starting to understand. There are maybe some new elements creeping into my thoughts and they may show up

Guy Maddin (left) and producer Greg Klymkiw snipping off "Johann's fingers" on the set of *Careful*, 1991. Photo by Jeff Solylo.

in the new movies, like the Winnipeg documentary, a thing where for the first time I'm really beginning to *feel* time's passage.

Melnyk I like the way you indulge your inner life so much. Most people don't do that. Most of us spend our time suppressing it. What you're doing for all the rest of us is you're expressing it even though you think it's just your imagination when it is really a collective psyche.

Maddin I very early on developed this idea that it was *the* job of a novelist, a good one anyway, to uncover for readers what they've been too frightened to uncover for themselves, to show them themselves somehow, even in some heavily disguised way, to provoke in that waking dream, which is them reading the novel, all the subconscious realizations they only have while sleeping.

Melnyk If you acted out this sort of stuff in real life, you'd get in trouble, right?

Maddin Well, that's the advantage of acting out this stuff in melodrama. In melodrama the characters get to do all the things that you'd get arrested, or at least socially censured, for doing in real life. You know, the way you get to sob loudly, scream, steal from, seize, hit, or even kill people in your dreams. You can do all the things that on some level you feel compelled to do, and when you wake up you're just yourself again. It's my noble responsibility as a melodramatist to show people what they really desire deep down.

Melnyk What about the new film projects you have?

Maddin I have a few. The most dismissible at the time we speak is *The Nude Caboose*. It's apparently meant to be downloaded on cell phones. I like the way cell-phone movies look. They look like a world viewed through a dirty aquarium: colourful, but murky, wonderfully murky, like a movie with algae! I've heard the demographic right now in 2006 for downloadable two-minute movies is thirteen-year-old boys. I think my movie is pitched more at nine-year-olds.

Melnyk What other ones are you doing?

Maddin There are two longer projects. *Brand Upon the Brain!* is going

I like the way cell-phone movies look. They look like a world viewed through a dirty aquarium: colourful, but murky, wonderfully murky, like a movie with algae!

to be playing at the Toronto Film Festival as a silent film event in the fall of 2006. It will have live music, three foley artists doing sound effects, a narrator, and a castrato singing operatic arias. It'll be fun for me. I managed to get my hands on a real castrato—not a papally decreed one, mind you, but one man who has turned his childhood medical misfortunes into a wondrous singing career. We're frantically editing that to get a picture lock two weeks from now. It's still only a rough assembly. My editor's working on it like crazy. John Gurdebeke, my tireless editor, working always, even while I'm napping. And then when we finish that we'll go on to edit the yet-untitled documentary on Winnipeg. It's already shot. I've got a number of pickup shots to do but I've done my little tour of Winnipeg and now we've got to figure out what we want to say with all this footage. But I know one thing for sure, once you finish the shooting—which sometimes sees one hundred people around you, helping you—after that, it's this cruel and lonely editing process, a monastic downshifting, which always causes an intense emotional crash within me. When I first started making movies, I worked completely alone as an editor. I went from seeing so many people every day to having all that just yanked away from me, suddenly stuck in a dark editing cubicle by myself, sorting through hours of rushes trying to decide if I even wanted to do this anymore. It got so lonely. I'm so happy to have John Gurdebeke do all that for me now. Now I can plan my movies knowing I will only have to do the fun part, John will do the rest. I may only be half a filmmaker now, but I'm the happy half.

Melnyk Any last thoughts?

Maddin You're from Calgary. I've never been there. Maybe I should go and do something on the Calgary Stampede. I know there's a whole gay stampede thing worth looking into. I'll bring Noam Gonick and he'll teach me how to e-mail the footage back to Gurdebeke!

I know one thing for sure, once you finish the shooting—which sometimes sees one hundred people around you, helping you—after that, it's this cruel and lonely editing process, a monastic downshifting, which always causes an intense emotional crash within me.

POSTSCRIPT

The foregoing interview was conducted in Winnipeg in the summer of 2006. In 2007 Guy Maddin moved to Toronto. The following was added in 2007.

Melnyk So you finally made the big move to TO. What caused you to do this?

Maddin I made my film about Winnipeg, it screened at home, and I was run out of town, practically in tar and feathers.

Melnyk What has it been like since you moved? Is your life what you expected it would be or is it different from your expectations?

Maddin I love it here. I'm near my daughter Jil and my granddaughter Ava. I get to have Sunday dinner with them without having to take an airplane over to their home. I still have the family cottage on Lake Winnipeg to sneak back to. No one knows me out there.

Melnyk In Winnipeg you were a big fish in a small pond, but here you aren't as big a fish. How do you deal with the competition?

Maddin No one ever noticed me in Winnipeg. No one notices me here. It's not exactly as I once dreamt it would be, but I actually like the way it's all played out. Everything is perfect.

MINA SHUM interviewed by Jacqueline Levitin

■

Levitin I know about your features, but I don't about your other stuff. How did you get involved in television—*Mob Princess*, *Shield Stories*, and *DaVinci's Inquest*? Is it just money making?

Shum It's craft. And it's actually a different beast than feature filmmaking. It's really strange actually. If you want to be a TV director, you kind of have to drop everything and be a TV director. And feature filmmakers are sometimes frowned upon in the TV world because we're feature filmmakers. We have got too much of our own opinion, and our own style. Basically, it takes a lot of time away from the feature work you are developing. So I only like to do a gig or two a year. Directing for hire is great because it's just pure craft.

Levitin Could you explain a bit more?

Shum In television the producers are really in charge and usually it's a writer-producer, so it's trying to figure out how my directorial vision can meld with their vision. I feel like I'm contributing to their work a little bit, but it's not really mine. I'm there to serve the producer, so it's completely different. You're honing your skills in terms of practising in different situations that my fantasy world wouldn't necessarily produce. In *Mob Princess* I shot a rape scene and it's great, but I would never write a rape scene. I write happy stories that make me laugh every day.

Levitin What was *Mob Princess* about?

Shum It's a TV movie based on a true story about a man who is sentenced for a mob murder and his daughter—fourteen years old—claimed he was wrongly accused and so, when she got older—when she was twenty-one—she started dating a mob member to try to get her dad out of jail, to find out who really did it. She had a husband with two children, in a completely domestic sort of suburban life, and yet at night she would go and be the mob girl and date this guy and try to get the information. I was interested in it because it's a double life, right? It's trying to lead the two lives. It is very different from *Long Life, Happiness and Prosperity*. My agent, Ralph Zimmerman, at one point said, "You've got to break out of the Chinese comedy stories, in terms of your reel." He is

In television the producers are really in charge and usually it's a writer-producer, so I try to figure out how my directorial vision can meld with their vision. I feel like I'm contributing to their work a little bit, but it's not really mine.

Opposite: On the set of *Long Life, Happiness and Prosperity*. (left to right) Nomi Peck, props master; Katia Stano, costume designer; Mina Shum; Peter Wunstorf, director of photography; Colin Leadley, first assistant director; Sarah Bjornson, art department draftsperson. Photo by Peter Wunstorf.

not saying that in terms of my *own* films, but in terms of getting other work, because I've been pigeonholed to the point that some producers are wondering if I even speak English.

Levitin That's surprising!

Shum I guess that's the kind of misconception that happens when you make films with Chinese faces.

Levitin What does your agent do—act as an intermediary?

Shum He goes and fishes for work for me. He'll negotiate a contract, and he will just keep putting my name up for projects and people either

take me or they don't. It's actually funny being your own writer-director, going from draft to draft and trying to make a movie. If you are actually trying to get work, you are out there competing with the people who have been directing television for fifty years. I haven't completely reconciled how I feel about all of it yet, because I like doing the work, but I don't like getting all riled up when there isn't any work. The feature film thing is so luxurious in a way because the responsibility is really to yourself and your audience.

Levitin Tell me about your new feature.

Shum It's called *The Immortals* and it's a kung fu comedy about a family who has been alive for 600 years, and they find themselves in Vancouver trying to run a restaurant unsuccessfully in Kits, and their only hope is that they can win this catering contract from the Chinese Business Association because their powers are weakening. Their *qi* has become imbalanced and the only way they can stay strong is to actually reestablish themselves in the community. Serve the mortals well. Maybe the way to serve the mortals is through their stomachs, they decide. And there is an evil immortal who has been chasing them for 600 years. So they are finally here, and they're trying to win this competition and the story is about Ling, who is the eighteen-year-old daughter in the family. She has been alive with her dad for 600 and he never listens to her. He never gives her the time of day. He treats her like she is eighteen, and she starts wondering if it would be better if she was just mortal—if she just stopped training, if she lost all her powers and just became like everyone else. And she meets a mortal boy at that point. So, it's sort of taking the coming-of-age story and fantasizing around it a little bit—the story that I'm so familiar with, which is "Who are you? Define yourself. How can you get love and respect from others if you don't love and respect yourself?" And my lead character in the story is a Taoist saint that no one believes in anymore. The story is about the family but everything hangs on Ling.

Levitin She is a Taoist saint? What does that mean?

Shum It means that you used to be mortal, and you are now immortal because you found the path through enlightenment. There is a set of immortals in Taoist folklore called the Eight Immortals, and they govern the arts. And there are stories about each of them. They basically were regular people who found the path to enlightenment and thus became immortal and could live forever. And they all acquired special powers. So, I sort of took that group and mooshed up all the stories and made them just a dysfunctional family whose powers are weakening in Vancouver.

Levitin They've moved here from China?

Shum Well, actually we chase them through time. To me it's an allegory

> The story I'm so familiar with is "Who are you? Define yourself. How can you get love and respect from others if you don't love and respect yourself?"

Opposite: Mina Shum on the set of *Long Life, Happiness and Prosperity* with director of photography Peter Wunstorf. Photo by Peter Wunstorf.

for the immigrant experience. Always on the run. I know from history where immigrants have landed. So I throw them into kitchens in various countries all throughout time. And the whole time they're being chased by this evil immortal, so they have to take off all the time. At one point they even end up hiding out in the Japanese internment camp. The daughter says, "Dad, we're not Japanese." "Yeah, but no one's going to look for us here." To me it's a commentary basically about being chased, because in a way, that's why people leave, right? They leave their original country because, for some reason, they don't feel that they can raise their children there. I just extrapolated and made the situation worse in my film, and they end up in Vancouver.

I love the Jackie Chan movies, and I love the Jet Li movies. I go see them. I like dance; I go see live dance; I love musicals. And I've always been trying to make a musical with Chinese people, but no one's bitten.

Levitin This relates to the Eight Immortals in Taoism. I know that you used Taoism also for *Long Life, Happiness and Prosperity*. So, have you been studying it?

Shum When I made *Long Life*, I was researching Chinese religions in general, and going to China all the time. So I kept visiting all the temples, because I think they're kind of neat and I am superstitious.

Levitin You're superstitious?

Shum My mother's superstitious, so I'm kind of superstitious. I like the idea that in Chinese religion "anything goes," in a way. We don't pray at the pulpit to one God. There are 6,000 gods. There are Eight Immortals, but there are dozens of other immortals. And the cool thing about the immortals is that they once were mortals as opposed to just being God, right? So in the world of theology, I think it was good that they did that because it made the supplicants aspire to something. We could become immortal if we found the path to enlightenment; if we practised compassion, moderation, and humility we could find the way. And maybe find immortality. But immortality is also just being in the moment, right? It is not hierarchal; it's for everybody. My primary interest in Tao is the idea of *qi*. On a film level, it is kind of neat that energy can be transferred from one person to another. For instance, in *The Immortals* there is a shape-shifter. The mother was a shape-shifter. She could change energies and take on other people's forms if she wanted to. Visually, bang! Wow, that's cool. She could become your enemy or your best friend.

Levitin Were you raised with any religion?

Shum Not really. We had the long life, happiness, and prosperity gods in our house but I didn't really know what they were until I got older. My father says he's agnostic because he went through such hell in the communist revolution. My mother says she believes in everything, just in case. So I think that rubbed off a little bit. Why not believe in everything?

Levitin You came here at the age of…?

Shum Nine months.

Levitin Nine months, from Hong Kong. So how long were they living in Hong Kong before coming here?

Shum My father came from Communist China, so he was in Hong Kong for about ten years. His family was aristocracy in China and they lost everything, so he took off one night because he was next. That was around '54 and then he met my mother in Hong Kong. My mother had already been living there since she was six. Their whole family had come from China; they weren't rich, and so nobody cared, basically. I think they had my brother right after they got married and then they came here. We came here.

Levitin So, how did you get into the kung fu part of your movie? Have you been interested in that?

Shum Well, I love the Jackie Chan movies, and I love the Jet Li movies. I go see them. I like dance; I go see live dance; I love musicals. And I've always been trying to make a musical with Chinese people, but no one's bitten. I needed something else, some other element to raise the stakes and create a slightly new genre for me. And *Kung Fu Hustle* was just coming out. I'd just seen *Shaolin Soccer.* I was talking to somebody about the idea and I thought, "I should give them kung fu powers!" And my friend went, "Oh my God, that's interesting!" So, it just spilled out of me after that. Even before I finished *Long Life*, I had been playing with the idea of Eight Immortals, and it was just so what I had done before. So, I wanted to sort of make it a bit bigger in scope, and at the same time not.

> My mother says she believes in everything, just in case. So I think that rubbed off a little bit. Why not believe in everything?

Because it's still really about this family, this girl trying to get her father to listen to her, right? But at the same time the stakes are completely different. It's about saving the world as opposed to saving yourself, right?

Levitin And they are fighting with these enemy immortals?

Shum Their chief enemy in the cooking competition is sending gangs and bad folks out—just regular problems being a restaurateur. You've got extortionists; you've got bylaws people. So that's one thing. On top of it, they've got this immortal situation that creeps into the story. It's a "cooking-fighting-dancing-extravaganza." That's what it is.

Levitin Dancing too?

Shum There is a tango competition in the middle. Because the community says, "All Chinese people have to know how to dance." Well, there is this whole ballroom tradition. And so the head of the community that's going to give the contract says, "Well, you know, if you want to get in with the community, you have to come and dance. Everybody does it." And the father, who has been so wounded from the death of his wife, refuses to dance because he doesn't want to shame her memory. And that's when the daughter and the father have the biggest fight. "I can't believe you are not willing just to dance. What are you afraid of?" "No one tells me what to do! Not this community and especially not you!" And they end up at this dance where the evil immortal shows up.

Levitin How did the Chinese community receive your films? How did it receive *Long Life, Happiness and Prosperity*?

Shum I screened it in Asian film festivals in America, and they loved it. Nobody knows these religions, so, like, nobody's going to be going, "Oh, I'm offended by something." With *Long Life*, people voted on which story they liked the best. That's what happens when you have a three-part story, right? "I like that story the best. I didn't like that person." But in general they were really pleased to see a working-class depiction. And they were just so happy to see their actors up there.

Levitin What does being Chinese mean to you?

Shum Being Chinese for me means that I can eavesdrop in two languages and that I have a whole other cultural lens to look at the world.

> Being Chinese for me means that I can eavesdrop in two languages and that I have a whole other cultural lens to look at the world.

So, for instance, I was out somewhere the other day having lunch with somebody but I couldn't concentrate on the lunch because there were two Chinese women nearby talking about boyfriends in Chinese. So part of my ear was over there—partly because I'm trying to get a gauge of what dating is like for them. Because I'm in the artsy world it's a bit different. It's a privileged place in a way. For research, I was completely taken because I wanted to know how it worked for them.

Levitin I still remember the line from *Double Happiness*, "My family, they're very Chinese…."

Shum Well, my family is very Chinese in a general sense. Traditional. Loyal to the family. They don't like to rock the boat. They like to fit into the community and stay fitted into the community because what people think is very important to them. That was a big thing when I was growing up. Mom was always trying to make me not stick out, and I was always sticking out all over the place. But for everything I just said, there are a million Chinese people who totally contradict that, right? The Chinese drag queen that does Marilyn Monroe is a complete contradiction to what I have just said. So it's partly just my growing up that affected my filmmaking.

Levitin So, when you go to China, how do you feel?

Shum I feel like a foreigner most of the time. If I keep my mouth shut, I'm still a foreigner, because I look different. My clothes are different. I carry myself with such authority that I have been mistaken for a guy in China. I don't think I carry myself with such authority, but there is a different way in which Chinese women handle themselves.

Levitin Does China make an impact on your filmmaking?

Shum Well, it's actually sort of something I deal with in *The Immortals*. The consumer society has completely taken over our spiritual beliefs in a way. "If I buy a Big Mac, I will feel better," as opposed to praying or finding some community connection. So I think that's one of China's biggest battles. Yes, they're a consumer society. At the same time, how do they hold on to some of that great loyalty, the roots, the community that they have that also gave them their strength. If everyone's just thinking for

> I carry myself with such authority that I have been mistaken for a guy in China. I don't think I carry myself with such authority, but there is a different way in which Chinese women handle themselves.

themselves, suddenly, it's completely the opposite of the communist ideal. So I think they're dealing with this rapidly building rift between the two ideals.

Levitin Where did you grow up? Where in the city?

Shum We switched houses every three years. That's how my parents tried to make money. They tried to flip real estate. So I've lived practically everywhere. I lived across from CBC when we first immigrated. Then we were at Britannia. Then we were at Cambie and 16th, and then Mission, BC, for five years. Then when we came back we were kind of in South Van, in the Fraser area. I went to John Oliver High School, and then we moved to New Westminster and that was the last house I was in with my parents. When I was eighteen I moved to 54th and Main into an illegal basement suite with a girlfriend I worked with.

Levitin You were pretty young! So is *Double Happiness* pure autobiography?

Shum I call it semi-autobiographical because if it was pure autobiography, which I think the first draft was, it would have been really boring. There would be long scenes where the father wouldn't talk to the daughter or ten-minute scenes where nothing would happen. Just the tension in the room, right? You fictionalize for film; it's not enough just to tell the events that occurred. And there is a whole bunch of events that didn't necessarily occur. My parents never set me up with a boy. But I knew of other girls that got set up with boys, so you kind of fictionalize and extrapolate.

Levitin And the girlfriend, was she there from the beginning?

Shum Oh yeah, I had a girlfriend like that through high school who was wiser, more daring, and more extroverted than I was.

Levitin How did *Double Happiness* develop as a script?

Shum I wrote the first draft to submit to the Canadian Film Centre Summer Lab Program in '91. Actually, that same draft got me into the Praxis Centre for Screenwriters, but by then I had already rewritten it. At the suggestion of Dennis Foon, my story editor, I basically wrote an entirely different movie and then realized that my movie originally was the right

> I call *Double Happiness* semi-autobiographical because if it was pure autobiography, which I think the first draft was, it would have been really boring.

movie. He was trying to push me to the edge. It was up to me to stand my ground and go, No! That was actually one of the most interesting things that have come from working with various producers in the writing process—knowing when to stand your ground. But from Dennis I learned the craft of three-act structure and the rhythms of a scene, although I had studied theatre. So, the rewriting was just sort of getting it into film form.

Levitin So, what is your background? Is it film and theatre?

Shum I did a theatre degree at UBC first. I did a BA and then I did a Film diploma. In high school I had been studying theatre. I did all the drama classes in high school, but I was already into directing plays in high school. And then in university I was mostly on the director's track. But there is no director's track when you do a BA. You take acting classes. There are two director courses at UBC. And I kept trying to get into film school the whole time. I was making little movies, and I was halfway through my degree when I realized I really wanted to be a filmmaker, not a theatre director.

Levitin At what point did you make *Me, Mom and Mona*?

Shum Right after I graduated film school. Actually, it was the second film after film school. I did a film called *Love In,* for which I got an Explorations Grant in '91, and then in '93 I shot *Me, Mom and Mona.*

Levitin Do you tend to work with the same crew all the time?

Shum Yes, on my films if I can. I tend to work with the same people over and over again. To me it is an ongoing piece of work. The second time I worked with Sandra Oh on *Long Life*, we were working on things that were a continuation of the things that we were working on in *Double Happiness* even though it is a different character. Like a director–actor thing: "How can I be such a crab to my daughter through all of *Long Life* and not play it as one note?" So Sandra and I developed this thing where I said, "Every time you yell at her you touch her, so that what you are saying physically is very different from what is coming out of your mouth," right? And that became a really nice little trait between her and the Mindy character in the film since she is always touching

I tend to work with the same people over and over again. To me it is an ongoing piece of work.

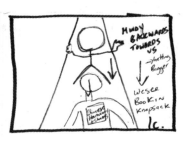

Above and *opposite*: Partial storyboards for Mina Shum's film *Long Life, Happiness and Prosperity*.

If you ever walked into the production office of anything I'm doing, there are always photographs all over the wall. There are paint chips every-where, and then I storyboard everything, too, on top of that. And shot lists.

her daughter even though she is always giving her shit the whole time. That is just a further extrapolation of working out physically emotional subtexts that we are doing in *Double Happiness*.

Levitin Let's go back to *Double Happiness*. You came up with the idea of the two sides of the colour palette for that one.

Shum Yes. From there, Michael Bjornson, the production designer—he's got a great sense of texture and palette and has worked on all my fea-tures—he and I decided that everybody should have a colour. Each of the family members should have a colour—partly because of the back-drops we did in the direct camera address. We needed to differentiate them and just give them their own texture. So we would literally go through paint chips. And I have in my library volumes and volumes of photographs, especially colour photographs, of various photographers I like, and any time I start a movie, I find a couple of shots that sort of exemplify how I think the film should feel. It may not have anything to do with Chinese people. It might be a photo of a clown, but something about it—this little corner of the photograph—that texture is the texture I'd like in my movie. If you ever walked into the production office of anything I'm doing, there are always photographs all over the wall. There are paint chips everywhere, and then I storyboard everything, too, on top of that. And shot lists.

Levitin Who are your other steady collaborators?

Shum I first met Peter Wunstorf, my director of photography, on the

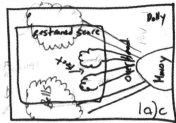
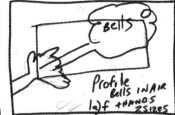

set of *The Grocer's Wife*, which was a UBC Master's film. Peter is a master of light; his eye is exquisite. He is a steady, artistic, soulful, quiet man. I'm crazy, passionate, loud, extroverted compared to him. So we yin-yang, right? And I made *Mob Princess*, *Drive She Said*, and *Double Happiness* with Steve Hegyes, the producer. Then there's people like Woody Lo in the art department—Hong Kong–born Chinese—who can write Chinese, can translate. When I'm not doing it right, because I'm not immersed in the community, he's there to gently tell me, "It's upside down." Then there's Les Ford, the assistant art director, who's been on all my films.

Levitin Tell me about Stephen Hegyes.

Shum He co-produced *Me, Mom and Mona*, and then he produced *Double Happiness*, so we have done four films together. I'd like to keep working with him. He did *Drive She Said*, but he had moved to LA during *Long Life* and so he wasn't available for that. Now he's come back and re-established. His family are immigrants from Hungary, so immediately there was this understanding of my sense of humour and how I saw the world—the outsider looking in. So creatively we just work really well together. At the same time there are these roots that are intertwined with our family upbringing. It's not just cultural. Our first love is our family. So that insight has always helped in terms of working. Even the *Mob Princess*, which was not a cultural story, but about a girl torn between her loyalty to her husband and her fascination with this mob world, was an easy discussion because we have similar backgrounds. Since we

I was reaching for themes and situations I had never shot before.

worked on so many films together he knows what I can do with something or what I *want* to do with something.

Levitin Where did *Drive, She Said* come from?

Shum It was partly a reaction to *Double Happiness*, which was so family oriented. I still think that it looks great. I cut my director's reel of *The Immortals* a couple of months ago [2006] and noticed that I included two things from *Drive!* Because there's some fantastic sequences in it. I think it could've probably used a rewrite before I went to camera with it, but at that point no one was there to tell me. Plus I was trying something different for myself, so it felt dangerous anyway. And it was dangerous, you know. I was reaching for themes and situations that I had never shot before, never really dealt with before. So it was great in terms of spreading my wings.

Levitin And *Long Life*?

Shum I'd written a Chinese musical called *Fry Girl* that no one would fund. So I spent a couple years on a project that ultimately didn't get made. It was about a Chinese girl who works at a McDonald's and has visions. She is ostracized from society. Everybody thinks she's a freak. And yet, she has musical visions that give her confidence in a situation. She fantasizes and so it's partly about reality—what is more real—what's going on in her head that boosts her confidence, or the horrible reality that's going on that gives her no confidence. I was working with songs from an artist named Ben Folds, trying to incorporate dance sequences into it. No one was willing to fund that.

Levitin If you had been able to get Sandra Oh to play the central character in *Drive, She Said*, as you had intended, you would still have had the Chinese element. Were you trying to keep in the Chinese stream with *Fry Girl* and *Long Life*?

Shum With *Fry Girl* less so, because it wasn't really about Chinese, it was about reality and fantasy. One of the struggles was a family struggle and she is rooted in what I know is a family story. They don't have to be Chinese; I could've made her white. In *Long Life*, it's the religion that sort of dictated that. And I wanted to do an ensemble piece. And some

> I spent a couple years on a project that ultimately didn't get made. It was about a Chinese girl who works at a McDonald's and has visions.

of the actors from *Double Happiness*, I wanted to work with them again. It's *Long Life, Happiness and Prosperity* in that order. It's very specific to the culture, those ideals.

Levitin Did you start looking into the religious aspects first and then write *Long Life*, or did you get involved with learning about the religion because you were making *Long Life*?

Shum I'd written a proposal called "Long Life, Happiness and Prosperity." Those are Chinese religious ideals. And then from there, I researched further what they meant. So, it was already steeped in the culture. I wrote the proposal during *Double Happiness*. Just before *Double Happiness* was made my dad lost his job before he was supposed to retire. And my mother said, "We came to Canada with less." I was immediately struck by that strong sense of spirituality. How could you not be in the dumps? So, that was my first tweak of *Long Life, Happiness and Prosperity*. That's all you need; that's all you want. And it's Long Life first because, if you live long, you can surpass any obstacle. And then Happiness is next because happiness is more important than money. I thought that was kind of interesting just in terms of the order of it all. I was to premiere *Double Happiness* in Toronto and I wrote the grant for *Long Life, Happiness and Prosperity*.

Levitin But then you did *Drive, She Said*?

Shum I wanted to do something not small and internal. I was reacting to the "nine thousand interviews" I did about *Double Happiness*. [*laughs*] I just wanted to do something different, and so I created a different place for my head to be, as opposed to mining my personal problems with my family again.

Shum And now you've got another story that goes back to Chinese roots. Do you think that you have more luck with your Chinese stories?

Shum It just depends on what I'm fixated about at a given time! And what I'm fixated about right now is the Immortals. I had written a script last year that I kind of got stuck on—about a girl that wasn't Chinese at all, just about a girl that couldn't get over the death of her mother. Couldn't move on. She was nineteen, and so she couldn't live life....

> It's Long Life first because, if you live long, you can surpass any obstacle. And then Happiness is next because happiness is more important than money.

Levitin Where does that come from?

Shum My dealing with death. That I'm getting older, and other people are dying, and I'm gonna die. It's weird because I was saying to another writer friend of mine, "*The Immortals* is the same film, I think, as the dead mother one that didn't work." It's just that it's much more fun to be in this world because they fight. And that they're immortals who are losing their moral compass, in a way. They're being affected as we are by all the different temptations. I'm an artist who is used to not making very much money. When you are measured by the way you look and what you own—and that seems to be the religion these days—how do you find your own moral compass within that to shun what everybody else says you should be? It's from my mother going, "Don't act that way. People will think this." And I would go, "Well, I don't care what people think." I think it would be great if all society cared a little less about what people thought. I think we would be able to just chill out a little bit more and realize what the important things are.

Levitin Do you have funding for this one yet?

Shum No. But I have a lot of interest, and I think it will be funded. I wanted to get the script to a point where it expressed all the things—because it's kind of complicated—all the things I want to express before I take it out there. I don't want go into the whole development field and start getting notes from people right away. Because of the television work, I have the luxury to self-develop. So, I'm in development.

Levitin Do you think there is a common theme that runs through all your films?

Shum I think so. A friend said to me after reading the draft of *The Immortals*, "Isn't it great that you keep doing the same movie, over and over again?" And I said, Yeah! The theme is "You have one life, so you have to live who you really are." It's funny, as I get older or younger, however it's working, I feel like that pressure to adhere to what other people think never goes away. It's just different codes, different sets of codes—code as a daughter, code as a wife, code as a person who is in the middle of their life, code as a senior.... It just never goes away, expectations of

> When you are measured by the way you look and what you own — and that seems to be the religion these days — how do you find your own moral compass within that to shun what everybody else says you should be?

who you're supposed to be, and what your dreams are, and what our values should be. [*laughs*] If we just valued, say, friendship—if that was what we valued the most, as opposed to money—there is no currency in that. You can't exchange that quality of time from a friend to another friend, or camaraderie. There is no way of actually quantifying that. Well, I say why don't we do that? Why don't we question what *is* the currency, what is our spiritual currency right now? But each person has to find that for themselves, right? I would love a world of nonconformists as opposed to people who don't fit in. I think I'm always examining that. That's why *The Immortals* is so potent for me as a story right now. The path of enlightenment is never static. You're never there—whatever that place is, you know, whether it's "I wanna be the best filmmaker in the world," well, I'll never get there. It's constantly evolving. It's gonna go up and down for the rest of my life until I can't make movies anymore. I think that's sort of a point of view I would like to promote in my work: "It's never static; it's always changing." So you go with the flow, and you have to make sure you speak up. You have to speak up because it's so easy not to be heard. So, it's always that to me, and it's always contemporary characters throughout my films who are doing that. I like to make people laugh. I don't think I could write a movie—I could probably adapt a book, but I could never write a movie from scratch—about a serial killer and his dark thoughts. It's just not where I want to be. The Buddhists say that your actions today determine your future, and I really believe that. What you fill you head with—I did an art installation in 2000 called *You Are What You Eat*—because everything you take in, everything you hear, it gets absorbed into you. I mean that's why we're all living in the post-9/11 world right now. That's all affected us a bit. So you have to be careful about what you are willing to let in. I do see a common theme. I know who I am. I'm not trying to be other people. We have our public face, what we need to present, to function in society, and then we have our secret desires. And I just think your secrets shouldn't be so secret. You should express yourself. You're gonna die. [*laughs*] ■

> Why don't we question what *is* the currency, what is our spiritual currency right now? But each person has to find that for themselves, right?

LYNNE STOPKEWICH

interviewed by **Kalli Paakspuu**

■

Paakspuu How did you finance *Kissed*?

Stopkewich The film was financed through family and friends and shot for $40,000. We got the equipment from UBC because it was my thesis film. We had a rotating crew because we couldn't pay them much and the actors worked for a reduced rate. The NFB donated film processing. The Canada Council came in with some finishing funds. BC Film gave us money for a 35 mm blow-up to go to the Toronto Film Festival. Once it screened there we sold the worldwide rights in one day. In film what happens is you "sell the film," but you don't get paid right away. You have to "deliver the film" with various elements to the distributor and that takes the better part of a year. So our final budget was more like half a million. In the end, the best part was when we paid back friends and family who had believed in the project from the very beginning.

Paakspuu What role did the William Morris Agency play in *Suspicious River*?

Stopewich After I made *Kissed* I signed with William Morris in LA. They have an independent film arm where they help package films and connect filmmakers with producers or distributors. Two producers in LA had bought the rights to the novel *Suspicious River* and had seen *Kissed*. Through a mutual friend they sent me the book to consider. I fell in love with it but they couldn't raise the money because they didn't have a track record. So I talked to my agent, Cassian Elwes, who was the president of the Independent Film Division at William Morris, and he put the package together whereby Hamish McAlpine, who was the British distributor for *Kissed*, invested in the film as the executive producer. His financing helped develop the script to the point where we could attach actors and attract distributors. That's basically how films are usually financed.

Paakspuu So the process with *Suspicious River* was quite different from *Kissed*?

Stopkewich The way I made *Kissed* allowed me complete creative control. I didn't have a distributor or Telefilm or anyone telling me who to

> The way I made *Kissed* allowed me complete creative control. I didn't have a distributor or anyone telling me who to cast, how to make the film, when to do it, or how to do it.

Opposite: Still from *Kissed*. Sandra (Molly Parker) with a corpse (Brian Pearson). © Boneyard Film Company Inc. Photo by Kharen Hill.

cast, how to make the film, when to do it, or how to do it. Looking back, I'm sure they would have been aghast at how we made *Kissed*—little by little, without ever having all the money to complete it. It took us about two years to complete and all the while, I was living hand to mouth. At one point we all had to stop working on the film, in order to go back to our real jobs and raise more money. It wasn't always fun, but at least I felt like I was sleeping in a bed of my own making.

Paakspuu Perverse sexualities often involve violence. What about violence in your films?

  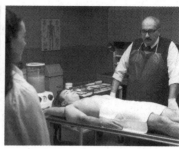

Above: Stills from *Kissed*. *Left to right*: Young Sandra (Natasha Morley) is fascinated by death; young Sandra with a friend enacting a death ritual; Mr. Wallis (Jay Brazeau) demonstrates embalming of a corpse (Noel Boulanger) to Sandra (Molly Parker); Sandra (Molly Parker) in the hearse (photo by Kharen Hill); Matt (Peter Outerbridge) shakes Mr. Wallis's (Jay Brazeau) hand over a corpse (Andrew Guy) while Sandra (Molly Parker) looks on (photo by Kharen Hill). Photos by David Ballard unless otherwise indicated. © Boneyard Film Company Inc.

Stopkewich The violence in my films happens, for the most part, off-screen. It's implied rather than depicted in a literal way. To me the sexuality isn't perverse sexuality, it is deviant sexuality. In other words, I don't want to label or judge it. It's not wrong, it's just different. That is why I make these kinds of films. I like telling stories that are "off the beaten track" of what we normally see in the theatres. That's what I am really drawn to myself. And I want to widen the scope of stories that are worthy of telling.

Paakspuu I read the book *Suspicious River* and I liked what you did with the characters of young Leila and the adult Leila by having the presence of the adult woman in the girl. How did you come across that idea?

Stopkewich The novel is quite dense and relentless compared to the film. I think it is one thing to read a book and imagine what's described, but quite another to be in a theatre, experiencing a filmic representation. To my mind, the film experience is much more visceral because you can't control it. Other than putting your hands over your eyes you are subject to whatever the filmmaker wants you to hear or see. That said, I felt that in creating a filmic translation of *Suspicious River*, less would be *way* more. I couldn't attempt a literal translation because it would be almost unwatchable. One of my earliest drafts contained a lot more of what is depicted in the novel—what happened to her as a child, her relationships with boys in high school, and then later on, her relationship

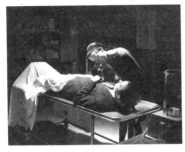  

with the local minister, who ends up raping her. If I had put all of that in the film, I don't think anyone would have stayed in the cinema until the end. So I realized, as I was writing, that I had to boil it down to the present-time storyline: Leila meeting Gary Jensen, what that triggers in her and why. The seeds of those "whys" would have been in her early childhood, so I decided to keep it to two time frames. In one draft I used flashbacks but that felt too disjointed, too much of an explanation and judgment. "Oh, that's why she is so screwed up. Because her mother was a whore or slapped around by her father and uncle." I prefer that the audience have a feeling of what might be going on but not make that literal a connection and therefore not judge the character and separate from her. That's when I came up with this idea of depicting Leila as a child in parallel time and not letting the audience know that until the very end of the story.

Actually, it wasn't even crucial if they ever understood that entirely. Even if they took the young Leila character as just "the little girl down the street," it's still impactful that the only character that adult Leila can talk to is a little girl she barely knows. So really, what is going on is that she is uncovering and remembering things about her past by having conversations with her younger self. Without this, I thought the extreme situations in the film would shut people down to Leila's experience. That they might, perhaps, feel like they had the character figured out and therefore they wouldn't be as engaged. This inclusion of the little girl

> I prefer that the audience have a feeling of what might be going on but not make that literal a connection and therefore not judge the character and separate from her.

(young Leila) opens us up, where adult Leila's extreme choices might shut us down.

Paakspuu You mentioned that Bergman's *Persona* influenced you.

Stopkewich Yes. I'm also a big fan of David Lynch because I think he is one of the few filmmakers who is still trying to push the cinematic narrative form. He experiments with space and time, casts different actors as the same character, plays with the notion of film "reality," etc. He likes to shake the audience up a little bit so that their film experience becomes much more dream-like—as though somehow you are inside the unconscious of the characters while you are watching the film. This is challenging and exciting to me.

Paakspuu I think you really went to the old myth of Leida and the Swan and you brought it into the forefront really early so that there is this burgeoning sexuality even from the very first scenes of the film.

Stopkewich Leila's deciding with whom and when she is going to have sex. She's realizing her sexuality is the last place where she can maintain some control of her life or not. As women, we're intrinsically and profoundly tied to our sexuality, and many times we are seen, or depicted, only through that lens. So, to use that power (or lack of power) as a way to work things out is a really common phenomenon among women, I think. When I read *Suspicious River*, it appealed to me not only because it is such an extreme story but because I could recognize myself and women around me in that character. Although most of us don't literally prostitute ourselves, nevertheless we have all been in unhealthy relationships or made self-destructive choices. Women seem to frequently internalize whatever is going on in their lives and turn it on themselves I think it's part of how we've been socialized—to take the back seat, to not ask for our needs to be met. So while I had a hard time understanding Leila's choices, I could relate to her emotional landscape. Originally, when I approached Molly Parker to play the part of Leila, she refused. She read the script and said, "Oh, God. Why do you have to make this film? It will be such a hard place for me to go as an actor and it's going

> When I read *Suspicious River*, it appealed to me not only because it is such an extreme story but because I could recognize myself and women around me in that character.

to be so draining. I don't know if I can do it." We sat there for a few hours and I talked to her about how I felt connected to it and why I thought it was an important story to tell. But she still declined. She had just finished shooting two or three features and was really exhausted. A few weeks went by and she phoned me back, "I can't get the story out of my mind. I'd really like to read the novel." So I mailed her the book and I knew from that moment she would be playing the part. It was just a matter of time....

Paakspuu So this is the second time you were able to use her talents.

Stopkewich Molly really gets inside the skin of those characters. It's amazing really. Who would really want to get into the skin of Leila? It's such a painful place to be, I imagine. So eventually I told Molly I was coming to Toronto to meet some other actors who wanted to play the part of Leila and everyone was very excited about the film. In truth, I had flown to Toronto to try and make my last bid to convince her to play the part but she didn't know that. I remember we met for breakfast and before we sat down she said, "Have you cast anyone to play the part of Leila yet? I've got to play that part." I just laughed and told her the truth. It was a phenomenal collaboration for me and helped me grow as a director. We've since discussed working together again because we both recognize that the level of trust we enjoy in our working relationship is sometimes an anomaly in the film industry.

Paakspuu Can you discuss Leila's desire for self-destruction and how you portray it in the film?

Stopkewich The climax of the film comes when Leila says, "Bring it on. I'm ready to die. I want to die. Kill me. In fact, I won't let you kill me, I want to kill myself *before* you can kill me." This is her position of power: choosing her own end. In a sense, she must kill herself in order to be reborn. So it appears that she is making bad choices, but in effect she *must* do this. To stay where she is and do nothing is worse than the path she is choosing. That is where her truth lies and she is compelled to go into it and have it consume her the metal is forged in the fire.

Paakspuu Leila's relationship to money is interesting. Generally when you have prostitution, there is a really strong connection with the money aspect but in her case it's like something that she doesn't know what to do with.

Stopkewich It's true. She doesn't. The money is almost inconsequential. Most people would say, "I'm saving up to get the hell out of this town." But on some level, Leila already realizes that she is trapped not by the town, but by her own history. She needs to break free of that and it's something which can't be bought. She needs to exorcise her demons and the money is a symbol of that.

Paakspuu I notice that you work a lot with your own autobiographical experiences, projecting them into the characters' worlds. For instance in *Kissed*, Sandra is a very Canadian girl and you brought in little elements of a Canadian girlhood into her world.

Stopkewich I still do that. I've been directing television for the past five years and I notice I bring those kind of details to bear there as well. I guess it's just how I work as a filmmaker. The details *are* the bigger picture. The trees *are* the forest…. For me, film is like memory—you have a feeling, you think you see the whole thing, but really it's all made up of specific, idiosyncratic moments frozen in time. In *Kissed*, things like the Birks blue box, the old-school Kotex napkins, the disco music played on a cassette recorder… these details *are* from my experience and they help personalize the film and make the character real….

Paakspuu I see that there is a big difference between a Lynne Stopkewich film and films directed by American directors in the same Canadian locales.

Stopkewich Americans are generally not trying to make those locales look like British Columbia. If they are, they tend to focus on the things that are most obvious to an outsider—the beauty of the landscape. However, my experience of BC is completely different. For the last twenty years I've lived in the Main and Hastings area, which is one of the poorest postal codes in Canada, where dozens of women have "mysteriously" vanished. I've not been drawn to "the beach" or "doing the Grouse Grind" or skiing at Whistler. I'm much more interested in the east side

---

> For me, film is like memory—you have a feeling, you think you see the whole thing, but really it's made up of specific, idiosyncratic moments frozen in time.

of the city, where people feel "more real" to me and I feel most at home. That is likely because I grew up in the east end of Montreal near the oil refineries. So my experience wasn't affluent or geared toward nature or recreation, but a much more working-class and urban one. Therefore, I think I try to tell stories about people that I can identify with and have populated my past.

Paakspuu So you identify with Leila's class interests and struggles?

Stopkewich Absolutely. She can't see beyond the town she's lived in her whole life. She intuitively recognizes that there is something more out there, but doesn't know what that is. And she also knows that if she doesn't take this rather dark path she will perhaps never break out of this place and it will ultimately kill her. People have asked me why. Why does she do these things? Why would you be interested in this story? It's largely because I see Leila as a really brave character. She's making a dangerous choice and jumping in the fire. She is following her instincts. Also, I like the image of the river in the story—that there is "another side"—a literal and symbolic place—that Leila can, and does, get to. This was my experience in moving to Los Angeles for a few years, which was after I made *Kissed* and I started writing *Suspicious River*. Like many filmmakers, I thought living at the "centre of the film world" would be fabulous. But it wasn't. I felt isolated and lonely and lost. In the end though, it *was* the perfect place to write a story about self-destruction and soul-searching. [*laughs*]

Paakspuu How do you work with others on a film?

Stopkewich Every project is different, but I like to take in as much information as possible from everyone, then make my own choices. I also like to work with the same people over and over again—lean on them creatively and jam it out. I tend to not immediately veto any wacky creative ideas and I love questioning everything. Sometimes, in the moment, I'm not the best listener, but if the suggestion is correct, it resurfaces. The funny thing about being a director is that everyone wants you to have all the answers all of the time, but sometimes you just don't. I tend to admit this but it doesn't always engender confidence in your

> I like to work with the same people over and over again—lean on them creatively and jam it out. I tend to not immediately veto any wacky creative ideas and I love questioning everything.

cast and crew. So basically, I always have an idea of what I want but like to remain open to other ideas when they come up. Then I go with my gut.

Paakspuu I've heard about a lot of filmmakers who have given their films to a distributor and have never seen any money.

Stopkewich You generally get paid an advance upfront but you rarely see anything else; that is, unless the film is really successful or the terms of your deal outline a cleaner split or favourable "corridor" to you. Most times, however, you will never see any money if you defer or hope to see profit in what's called "the back end." That is because some distributors cite all the expenses which need to be paid out first, and most filmmakers don't have the time or financial resources to ask for an audit. Also, it's rare for a Canadian film to make back in the theatres what it cost to originally produce. In any case, regardless of your financing or distribution deals, my advice to aspiring filmmakers is to make films for the right reasons and make the best film you can.

■

Melnyk Could you provide some biographical information about yourself and your life in Calgary?

Burns I was born and raised in Calgary in Westgate near Westbrook Mall. My parents are British immigrants, who moved to Calgary in the '50s. I grew up in what was a new suburb at the time.

I'm so critical of suburbs in my work but I think I had a really happy childhood. We actually had a cabin just outside of town, where we'd spend summers. My parents are both from Liverpool, who grew up in teeny houses where there would be like twelve people in a very cramped environment. We'd go there on holidays when I was a kid. I was the only one in the family born in Calgary. As I started growing up, I started wishing I'd grown up maybe there, because of a vibrancy that was missing from where I lived. I started thinking there's something wrong with suburban living, and my future was going to be that of a house painter like my dad. Then I got this idea when I was like twenty that I was going to go to this clothing college in Montreal called LaSalle College. I was going to go into fashion, but I wasn't going to take design; I was going to take production. So I ended up doing time studies for a little while. Then I got a job in Kelowna working for a company producing T-shirts. By this time I had actually bought a big typewriter and tried writing scripts. I went to a scriptwriting class in which I was the only student. I was in my mid-twenties. Calgary didn't have a film school so I enrolled at U of C and took Fine Arts. I was a mature student who started out in art. But I realized that it was probably a better idea to be in drama, so I transferred to drama, and the year I transferred to drama I applied to Concordia, because I heard when I was in Montreal doing the fashion thing that there was a film school there. I just loved Montreal. I got a letter back from them saying that you're not getting in and you're not even close to getting in. I was like twenty-eight, so the next year I applied again but I flew to Montreal for the interview. I had some poems and a couple of drawings. You weren't expected to have any video or film under your belt like today. I went to the interview, and I remember someone asking, "Well,

> As I started growing up, I started wishing I'd grown up maybe there [Liverpool], because of a vibrancy that was missing from where I lived. I started thinking there's something wrong with suburban living.

you're a pretty good at drawing. Why don't you just want to do that?" But somehow I convinced them that film was for me and they let me in.

Melnyk How did film school go?

Burns It was great. My production teacher was talking about *Slacker*, which had just come out. I saw it in Montreal and I remember thinking that this film looks like a film school film—technically rough, actors not very good—and I thought that I can do this. It was conceptually complex but technically it wasn't. It broke the mystique of having to go to Hollywood to make films. It looked like a student film but people were paying to see it in the theatre. That was a huge thing for me. There were other films that affected me in this same way. *Strangers in Paradise* had this same feel to me. Then I made my second-year short. Because I had worked in construction I had more money than a lot of other students for my films. I got a student loan even though I didn't need the money and I used that money for my film as well. The other students were making films for $500, but I made a twenty-minute film with actors and a bus I rented from the city. Part of it came from my being thirty, so I knew how to do things. I spent $7,000 and it won best second-year film. That came with a cash award.

The film is called *Happy Valley*. It's basically *The Suburbanators* with just two Arab guys. Because I had a drama background, I went to the National Theatre School to get actors instead of just using friends. I ended up making a "foreign-language film" with no subtitles. Basically, even if the performances aren't perfect, it doesn't matter, because you don't understand it. They were Arabic because I just figured there was less chance that someone in my audience of film students spoke that language. So two Arab guys walk across town to visit a friend, but when they get there they go in the wrong house. They go into the wrong house and just as they realize their mistake the people that really live there come home. So they go hide in the back of the house and then sneak out. That's the whole movie.

Melnyk You had a script?

Burns I had a script, which I wrote in English. The actors translated it

Slacker was conceptually complex but technically it wasn't. It broke the mystique of having to go to Hollywood to make films. It looked like a student film but people were paying to see it in the theatre. That was a huge thing for me.

into Arabic. At the screening everyone's laughing at the right things, like, everyone gets it. That was the biggest boost for me. So I came out of Concordia with this award, but I also had this film. The Director's Guild of Canada and Telefilm had this program for recent graduates of film schools, so I sent them my film, which I had just finished, and said I want to do basically the same film but in colour. They were giving out five $10,000 grants. I didn't have a very good proposal but they liked my student film enough to give out five $9,000 prizes instead and give me the five they skimmed off the other prizes. So within a few months of getting out of school, I was making another short, which I called *Beerland* and it was basically *Happy Valley II*. Before I even finished that film I applied to Canada Council to do *The Suburbanators*, based on *Happy Valley* by adding two more storylines with young Caucasian guys.

I got out of school in '92, and made *Beerland* in the fall of '92. I probably wrote *Marlborough Mall*, which was what *The Suburbanators* was called originally, over the winter of 1992–93 and shot it in the fall of 1994. It got into the Toronto International Film Festival a year later.

Melnyk *The Suburbanators* had an initial budget of $25,000. Was that Canada Council money?

Burns I got twenty from Canada Council and five from the Alberta Foundation for the Arts.

Melnyk What did it end up costing?

Burns To finish it to film for Toronto it ended up at around $65,000. After TIFF it got picked up for Sundance. That was big. It made something like $10,000 in one week in a theatre in Calgary and we used our percentage of the box office to pay for the trip to Sundance. It was really unbelievable…. When we were in Toronto, some guy at a party told me that I should have another script ready for Sundance, which is only four months later. So I wrote *Kitchen Party* between Toronto and Sundance in those four months. I'm not sure how I actually came up with the idea. Because I was a fan of *Slacker* and I'd seen *Dazed and Confused* I was probably ripping off Richard Linkletter's second film. Part of it was that I was comfortable making a film about something I knew. *Suburbana-*

The Suburbanators got picked up for Sundance. That was big. It made something like $10,000 in one week in a theatre in Calgary and we used our percentage of the box office to pay for the trip to Sundance.

tors was about doing nothing, which I'd been good at in my twenties. *Kitchen Party* was about peer pressure, which was something we're all familiar with. So it was a teen comedy but something different from your standard Hollywood teen comedy where everybody learns something. I wanted to make an anti-teen-comedy where there are no lessons, and where the main character's a jerk, who doesn't get the girl. I just kind of went against the conventions of that genre. I went to LA with it after Sundance. But they basically said it's too smart for a teen comedy. They told me to dumb it down into a teen party film. I thought we could make it in Canada the way I wanted it made. So we came back, but going to Telefilm Canada is a lot different than going to the Canada Council, which just gives you a grant. It's just a lot more complex. You need a distributor. You need to pre-sell it to TV and there's tax credits, etc. Telefilm knew that we were in trouble, so they introduced us to a group in Vancouver, who were the line producers of *Hard Core Logo*. They were looking for another project, which Telefilm knew so they introduced us. That's how it came together. Within a year of premiering *Suburbanators* I was shooting *Kitchen Party*. It came together very fast.

Melnyk What was it like shooting in Vancouver?

Burns It was really not a pleasant experience. *Suburbanators* was my movie. I could just do whatever I wanted. I tried the same approach when I made *Kitchen Party*, but the producers there wanted a say. It was a learning curve for me and we had a huge conflict. But when it premiered in Toronto there were actually people from Miramax and New Line saying to us, "You'll get an offer, you'll get an offer!" In the end no one bought it because Harvey Weinstein didn't like it enough. He said he liked it a lot but he didn't love it. So it had theatrical distribution in Canada and sold around the world for TV. It had a production budget of $1.5 million, standard for a Canadian movie of the time [1996].

Melnyk What did you do at that point?

Burns I wrote another script. Nobody liked it. It was more of a genre picture, more of a thriller, and it wasn't well written. At the time, when I was writing it, I had a friend in Telefilm. I phoned him up and told him I was

Suburbanators was my movie. I could just do whatever I wanted. I tried the same approach when I made *Kitchen Party*, but the producers there wanted a say. It was a learning curve for me and we had a huge conflict.

looking for a new producer since I'd had a falling out with the other guy I'd worked with. He suggested Shirley Vercruysee. She'd never produced a movie, but had related experience. So we started working together on this script of mine that wasn't going so well. In the meantime, I applied to Canada Council to do this one-shot video about the Plus 15 system in Calgary. The Plus 15s are heated walkways between downtown office towers in Calgary that are 15 feet above street level. It's an architectural component of Calgary's downtown that I thought was destroying the downtown. It was supposed to be one shot over one lunch hour. While I was writing it, I heard about the *Time Code* video that was doing just that and more. So I dropped that idea.

I teamed up with James Martin to write the script. At that time Telefilm was in this cyclical thing, where you literally had to have all your pieces together by something like February 1st—distributor, etc. We'd missed the date so the only way to make a film that year was if we made something super low budget. The distributor from *Kitchen Party* really liked the script for what became *waydowntown*. Originally we were thinking we would make the film for something like $200,000, but the budget kept going up, first to $400,000 and then to a little over around $700,000. I got a producer credit on the film mostly because it was Shirley's first film and I made some suggestions here and there, but Shirley produced the film.

We wrote it January and February of '99. I was doing what I wanted again without any interference. I could just do what I wanted. We shot it downtown and it was a lot of fun. It won Best Canadian Film at TIFF in 2000.

Odeon distributed it. It was great working with video, but it's a myth that it's some huge saving. Blow-ups at the time were very expensive. Plus there's the myth that you can shoot forever because tape is cheap. But a day is only so long and you still have a big crew there and the actors are all ACTRA so as usual time is always tight. I wasn't always ready for the next shot as much as I like to be.

Melnyk *waydowntown* made your reputation, didn't it?

Opposite: Laurie (Paulo Costanzo) and Dot (Emily Hampshire) at the subway (from *A Problem with Fear*). © Fear Alberta Ltd. Photo by Dan Power.

Burns It was my most successful film to that point. It's probably the film more people know about…. It's funny because it came out of an idea of just making a film about the Plus 15. To me, it's all about architecture in the downtown core.

Melnyk Do you think you have injured your career by continuing to live in Calgary?

Burns Telefilm and Canada Council like the regional. They want to spread their money around. At least that was something I always thought was to my advantage, but, who knows, maybe I was just using that idea to rationalize staying here. I was certainly known as the guy from Calgary for the first couple films, so it really helped from that point of view.

Melnyk So you stayed in Calgary and made *A Problem with Fear*. How did that go?

Burns It started out as the theme of the script that I couldn't get made. It was about this guy in Banff, who was an agoraphobe. In retrospect, I should've gone back to the story and done that, but after *waydowntown* I wanted to do it again downtown because for me that's the best set in the world. So I turned it into an urban story. But the original script was wacky. The city had its own brain, a supernatural quality. But then I got involved in this crazy thing that they love here in Canada, which is the story editor. I just got sucked into it. Your movie needs this, this, this, and this. It just became a different movie. I wrote the script with my wife, Donna Brunsdale, and she was reluctant to go along with a lot of the story editing but I pushed ahead. The script we liked at the beginning got sucked into a vortex and never came back out. I've turned against the story editor idea since then. Sure you need comments from people. But my scripts have never fit very well into the formula of the three-act, plot turn here and there model. Without a pre-sell to TV, you can't make your film. If they don't like it, you don't make it. So you're basically pandering to TV tastes, and they love the story editor.

I remember just a couple of months before shooting thinking I should just stop, because I don't even know what this movie's about anymore. But it's hard to stop the train once it's left the station. There's

> I got involved in this crazy thing that they love here in Canada, which is the story editor. I just got sucked into it. Your movie needs this, this, this, and this. It just became a different movie.

still okay moments in it, but things critically didn't work out well. Basically my first three features were well reviewed so it was hard to get kicked down a few notches. We went to Toronto and the weeklies came out panning it. I had these two big TV things to do and it kind of just took my mind off the situation. You feel bad for everybody that worked on it and all the effort put into it.

Melnyk So you moved onto *Radiant City*?

Burns What was great about Radiant City was that it helped me get my confidence back after getting beaten up over *A Problem with Fear*. I co-directed it with Jim Brown. Jim and I talked about it at a New Year's Party we had, and decided to meet and try doing something together. It was a subject I was really interested in, like the Plus 15s in *waydowntown*. Calgary is defined by suburban sprawl. It was fun, really great fun. The NFB got on board right away; so did the CBC. We had some conflicts here and there with the broadcaster who basically dumped it. But aside from that, it was a great experience and Jim and I are working on another doc together.

Melnyk Do you still view the world much as you did when you began making films?

Burns Yes, I think so. My stuff has always been a bit cynical. My interests are in social commentary and that's how I serve the community in some sense. It's how I've branded myself as well, I guess. I'm not sentimental and my stuff is not generally fodder for Hollywood. I do things a certain way and I want it that way. I just don't have the sensibility for Hollywood—I'm not into happy endings.

Melnyk Alberta does not produce a lot of film directors. Why not?

Burns I always wonder about that. It's not just Alberta; it's the whole country. Where are all the movies the digital revolution promised? The problem is that the technology doesn't make you a storyteller. That's the hard part. I'm always surprised by how few people are coming up behind me. Certainly it's hard to break into the bigger-budget ranks but the film co-ops alone are such great facilities for being able to get the low-budget stuff done. Maybe I'm just focused on who's ahead me, and I don't see the throngs of feature directors coming up behind me.

> Where are all the movies the digital revolution promised? The problem is that the technology doesn't make you a storyteller. That's the hard part. I'm always surprised by how few people are coming up behind me.

Right: The Moss family on the set of *Radiant City*. © Sprawl Alberta Ltd. Photo by Donna Brunsdale). *Opposite*: Tom (Fabrizio Filippo) flying on the set of *Flying 2*. © 848296 Alberta Ltd. Photo by Darrell Lecorre.

Certainly when you look at the Toronto Film Festival there are only a small number of slots for first-time filmmakers. A lot of the slots are taken by established directors, because people who already have the reputation will get in more often than not. So there's room for maybe three or four first features, if that. On the other hand, it's not like you hear about all these really great first features that didn't make Toronto. No, there aren't any.

Melnyk What about the future?

Burns When I got into this I was looking for a job that I would look forward to doing when I got up in the morning. I wanted something I was going to do for the rest of my life. It's a job, and you have to do it every day, and it's what you want to do every day. I've been very lucky. There aren't many people that have the opportunity to do what I do. If I can keep plugging away at making a film now and then I'll be happy.

When I got into this I was looking for a job that I would look forward to doing when I got up in the morning. I wanted something I was going to do for the rest of my life.

ANNE WHEELER EDITING *GREAT GRAND MOTHER*, HER FIRST FILM ABOUT WOMEN OF THE EARLY WEST

■

She's one of Canada's defining English-language cinematic voices. During her career she's directed eight feature films, nine movies for television, and numerous documentaries, miniseries, and television episodes. Her movies for television have been nominated for a total of thirty-one Geminis and her films for a total of thirty-eight Genie Awards. As François Truffaut wrote in *Hitchcock*, directing films requires "multiple and often contradictory talents ... only a mind in which the analytic and synthetic are simultaneously at work can make its way out of the maze of snares inherent in the fragmentation of the shooting, the cutting and the montage of a film."

Wheeler trained as a mathematician, musician, and music teacher before directing her first film. When she talks about directing she uses musical analogies and notations. And when she shoots, it's with mathematical precision. At our first meeting in 1998 to discuss working together on *Better Than Chocolate,* producer Sharon McGowan

Wheeler trained as a mathematician, musician, and music teacher before directing her first film. When she talks about directing she uses musical analogies and notations. And when she shoots, it's with a mathematical precision.

Anne Wheeler on the set of
Edge of Madness.

and I arrived at Anne's office to the sound of delicate piano playing. It was Anne. When we asked her what the piece was, she said it was her morning improvisation; each day begins with one. I think that this ability to start fresh, to reinvent, is a hallmark of her work as a film artist.

Wheeler's body of work harks back to classic auteurs, directors like George Stevens, Akira Kurosawa, and Billy Wilder whose themes and styles embraced all genres: westerns, comedies, film noir, drama. Wheeler is the same: whether it's the social-issue drama of *Loyalties*, the romantic naturalism of *Bye Bye Blues*, the neo-noir of television's *Da Vinci's Inquest*, or the romantic comedy of *Better Than Chocolate*, Wheeler's recurring themes of liberation and self-knowledge run through them all.

Like George Stevens, Wheeler is a director who understands the importance of landscape in relation to the psyche. Stevens's westerns *Shane* and *Giant* share with Wheeler's Alberta films the metaphor of western place. Land and sky become a tabula rasa on which deeply internalized characters (male and female) can see themselves in a new light. Like Akira Kurosawa, another director who understood westerns, Wheeler isn't afraid of epic pacing, and, like Billy Wilder, whose comedies stressed character exaggeration, Wheeler's forays into comedy (*Better Than Chocolate*, *Suddenly Naked*) prove that she too can handle an "everywoman" protagonist thrust into a cockeyed universe.

Wheeler isn't afraid of epic pacing, and her forays into comedy prove that she can handle an "everywoman" protagonist thrust into a cockeyed universe.

In the 1970s and '80s Wheeler collaborated with the National Film Board making documentaries and short dramas such as *Great Grand Mother*, *Augusta*, *Happily Unmarried*, *Teach Me to Dance*, *One's a Heifer*, *A Change of Heart*, and *A War Story*. The latter, narrated by Donald Sutherland, explores her father's experiences as a doctor in a Japanese prisoner-of-war camp during World War Two. These films laid the groundwork for the films to follow.

Her first feature film, *Loyalties* (1986), starred Tantoo Cardinal and Susan Wooldridge and was written by Sharon Riis. *Loyalties* is a powerful film about a friendship between a Metis and a British woman, and deals with child abuse and how a case of abuse (the British woman's husband assaults the Metis woman's daughter) propels the two women to action. This groundbreaking film moved Wheeler into the international narrative film world and won awards at film festivals in Houston, San Francisco, Toronto, Portugal, South Africa, Montreal, and the Grand Prix at the Créteil International Women's Film Festival in Paris.

Bye Bye Blues (1988) was inspired by her mother's war years as a musician in a small dance band, and established Wheeler as an auteur director. We explore the making of *Bye Bye Blues* in this interview. In 1990, she directed the adaptation of the classic novel *The Diviners*, by Margaret Laurence, for CBC Television. The novel was adapted by renowned screenwriter Linda Svendsen. "Writing is a form of divining," Laurence has famously said, and with *The Diviners* Wheeler develops what is now becoming her major theme—women's struggles to discover and divine self-knowledge.

The War Between Us (1995), another film for CBC Television, explores the Japanese internment in Canada during World War Two and is again a film about the bonds between women. This film was written by screenwriter Sharon Gibbon, the granddaughter of the lead character. As with so many of Wheeler's films, real life is once again "divined" into fiction. The film garnered international awards, including the Special Jury Prize from the Houston Film Festival, the Red Cross Award for Humanity, the Critic's Choice Award at Monte Carlo, and a Cable Ace Award for Best Foreign Programming in the United States. In 1996 Wheeler wrote and produced *Mother Trucker: The Diana Kilmury Story*, directed by Sturla Gunnarsson. The film is a biopic about the woman who fought to change corruption within the Teamsters. That film won the Cable Ace Award in the United States for Best International Programming. In 1998 Wheeler directed the first three episodes of *Da Vinci's Inquest*, setting the style for the gritty hit series. *Better Than Chocolate* (1999), our lesbian-themed romantic comedy, premiered at the Berlin Film Festival and was a critical and commercial success. The film received wide distribution in the United States, playing in over 300 theatres. We discuss our collaboration on this film in

"Writing is a form of divining," Laurence has famously said, and with **The Diviners** Wheeler develops what is now becoming her major theme—women's struggles to discover and divine self-knowledge.

the interview. *Marine Life* (2001), adapted from the linked short stories by Linda Svendsen, also explores Wheeler's primary themes of families headed by women and the discovery of self. In 2000 Wheeler directed *Suddenly Naked*, a romantic comedy that also premiered at Berlin and, through humour, questions what happens when artists create for fame and fortune rather than express themselves truthfully.

On the set of *The War Between Us*. Local residents who were related to those who were interned played extras in this drama about Japanese Canadians during World War Two.

For the purposes of this interview I focus on two of Wheeler's feature films: *Bye Bye Blues*, a story rooted in her family and place of birth, and *Better Than Chocolate*, a film rooted in my family and place of birth. But to begin, I ask her about getting started in the film world.

Thompson Your first major film *Great Grand Mother* [1976] was a documentary about women who settled the Canadian West. What does the West mean to you?

Wheeler The West and more specifically the Prairies have always been a source of inspiration for me. The endless horizon symbolizes the endless possibilities. I grew up in Edmonton, but both of my parents came from the country, and one aunt had a farm north of the city where I kept my Appaloosa mare. As a child, I felt safe and would ride alone for miles in any direction. If there were fences, I could always find a gate. The experience of being alone, with no one watching or judging, allowed me to just "be there" in the moment, to enjoy and absorb what was wild and real.

Thompson You've been working as a director for almost three decades. What's kept you going?

Wheeler My sense of curiosity, I suppose. And a sense of purpose. It started with *Great Grand Mother,* a small documentary that led me into

> An aunt had a farm north of the city where I kept my Appaloosa mare. As a child, I felt safe and would ride alone for miles in any direction. If there were fences, I could always find a gate.

the personal lives of women who had never been asked about their stories. They had come to this wilderness to settle the land, many of them naively and, in doing so, they discovered their own capabilities. Many gave up. Others died trying to survive. The research unearthed a multitude of stories that had never been told, stories that would have been lost and forgotten. It was fascinating to hear of their experiences and I came to have a tremendous respect for those who had gone before me.

Thompson How did *Bye Bye Blues* [1988] come to be?

Wheeler In the late '70s I started out to make *A War Story* [1981], which was to be about my parents. It amazed me that they were separated for

Opposite: 1979. Anne in front of a poster for *A War Story*, a feature documentary, narrated by Donald Sutherland, about her father's experiences as a doctor in a prisoner-of-war camp. *Above*: cast on the truck during the filming of *Bye Bye Blues*. Photo by Doug Curran.

more than five years during World War Two, when my father was in a Japanese prisoner-of-war camp. They had met as children on the Prairies, married, and went to India in the '30s, where my father was a doctor. When the war broke out he was assigned to a division from India and my mom came home to the Prairies. They were reunited late in 1945, and I was born ten months after dad's return. Both of them had changed significantly yet the commitment, without question, remained. I was a child of the '60s, a time of "free love" and "no strings attached." Their relationship was not uncommon amongst their peers, but the definition of marriage was now being questioned. As I worked on *A War Story*, I met many of the men with whom my father had been interned, most of them Scottish or Welsh. He had never seen any of these fellows since they had parted ways more than thirty years before this. I became consumed by my father's story and their stories, and that whole theatre of war, where East met West, and their worlds collided. It was thought provoking and so little had been written about it. So, my mother's story was put on hold. Almost ten years later, the time was right for me mount a substantial feature, and I chose to go back to what I had put aside, but I would make a fictional drama, inspired by what she had experienced.

Thompson Why a drama?

Wheeler I felt the limitations of documentary filmmaking with *A War Story*. Often you are bound by your research and personal connections. I felt protective of my parents. And when I took a group of men back to where the camp had been, I felt exploitive. For me, they were going back to hell. I couldn't push them to tell me what I already knew in some ways. It was horrendous what they had endured, and now I was forcing them to relive what they had spent most of their lives trying to forget. As a filmmaker, I felt I was telling the story from the outside looking in, and I wanted to reverse that situation. Because my mother was still alive, and my father died when I was young, I had a much better sense of who my mother was, and what the experience had meant to her. Still I approached *Bye Bye Blues* as though it was a documentary, interviewing many women who had gone through World War Two alone. Many

> I approached **Bye Bye Blues** as though it was a documentary, interviewing many women who had gone through World War Two alone. Many had done things they'd never thought they were capable of doing.

In *Bye Bye Blues* the distances between people and places is a metaphor for the distances between them spiritually and emotionally.

had done things they'd never thought they were capable of doing.

Thompson What for you is the theme of *Bye Bye Blues*?

Wheeler A person awakening to her own strength. The ongoing consequences of war.

Thompson There's a lot of imagery and shot construction of the heroine in the vast expanse of the Prairie. Can you elaborate on that?

Wheeler In *Bye Bye Blues* the distances between people and places is a metaphor for the distances between them spiritually and emotionally. Every generation goes through an evolution, and in *Bye Bye Blues* Daisy represents an emerging breed of women, so different from her parents. She has travelled and knows about the world beyond. Because of her circumstances she is forced to return to where she was born, to live with her parents, and of course the wilderness becomes her prison.

Thompson Music is also a force for liberation in the film.

Wheeler From the time I can remember, my mother played and our

Working with Kate Reid on the set of *Bye Bye Blues*. Photo by Doug Curran.

There is no point listing a series of events that happens in a lifetime if you can't abstract some meaning from those experiences. To distill that meaning takes time.

family gathered around the piano to sing. Others danced. Music is a big part of our relationship. I was four years old when I realized I could find the harmony in any song and sing it effortlessly. It was a gift, and I always felt so lucky to be able to perform with her, which we did for years. We sang together, played together. I always felt closest to her when we were making music.

Thompson Although Daisy is liberated in the film through music and romance, it's her husband she stays with.

Wheeler Yes. I'd been moved by the sacrifice my mother made for the family. She was talented and beautiful, and yet her own ambitions did not fit well with her circumstance. Think of it. She could not have known *who* would come home after five years, but she remained faithful to the core. That's who she was. She was naïve about what he had experienced, like everyone was at the time. But she was his wife and mother of his children. They were childhood sweethearts, and in the end she made a choice that many today would not make [to give up her personal dream] but she couldn't have lived with herself had she done otherwise. And she never expressed any regrets to me, but I could see the delight she felt whenever she sat down to play.

Thompson How long did it take you to write the script?

Wheeler Three years. The first draft started with my parents' childhood friendship. With draft after draft I got down to the heart of the story. There is no point listing a series of events that happens in a lifetime if you can't extract some meaning from those experiences. To distill that meaning takes time.

Thompson Is the film an epic?

Wheeler Epic? It's a small word for something big. Some would say it's an epic—extraordinary in size and scope, starting in India, ending in Alberta on the cusp of a new age. But I want the audience to feel it is about someone not unlike themselves, caught up in events bigger than their world. It is a personal film, a romance, and in some ways a tragedy.

Thompson I'd like to explore your relationship with the producer of *Bye Bye Blues*, Arvi Liimatainen.

Epic? It's a small word for something big. Some would say it's an epic—extraordinary in size and scope, starting in India, ending in Alberta on the cusp of a new age.

Opposite: Luke Reilly and Rebecca Jenkins in *Bye Bye Blues*. Photo by Doug Curran.

Wheeler Arvi and I have worked together many times [*Cowboy's Don't Cry, Bye Bye Blues, Angel Square*, and *Marine Life*] and consider each other family. We weren't always close. For a time we both lived in Edmonton, but we were not on the same path. He was doing a number of shows with American producers, breaking into that market, and I was a devout Canadian documentary filmmaker who made films, mostly for the National Film Board. There was no specific conflict; we just didn't connect.

Then I was asked to make *Cowboys Don't Cry* [1988], produced by Janis Platt, and she asked me who the best line producer for the film would be, and I honestly had to say "Arvi." He laughed when I asked him. Then he said yes and we never looked back. The last film we made together was *Marine Life* in 2001.

Thompson The shoot for *Bye Bye Blues* involved two continents and two seasons. Tell me about it.

Wheeler The shoot was thirty-two days in total, I believe. We had a twenty-day summer shoot—half of it in Drumheller and half in the brand-new Allarcom Studios in Edmonton. Then we went to India for a chaotic six-day shoot. We only took twelve people to India, so most of the crew there was local. When we left India to come home, we had trouble with customs and had to leave our footage behind, so it was almost two months before I knew if the footage was all right. That was stressful. But overall, the making of *Bye Bye Blues* was fantastic. Hugely rewarding on all levels. I had a freedom, never again experienced, to simply go for it. We built a farm on the lip of the valley outside of Drumheller (designed by John Blackie, with whom I have worked time and again) and three dance hall sets. The new studios were a symbol of what we hoped was going to happen in terms of production in Alberta. Dr. Allard [the television station owner who built the studios] was there most days, watching from the shadows, as we initiated the space. We felt like the whole city, the province, was behind us. The support was overwhelming.

Thompson How do you work with actors?

> We felt like the whole city, the province, was behind us. The support was overwhelming.

I often work with each actor separately so that the other actors don't necessarily know what is going to happen—they will have to react to what is new.

Wheeler I like to work one-on-one. Rarely do I have the opportunity to rehearse, and, quite frankly, unless it's a love scene or a fight scene or something that needs to be planned for safety and expediency, I'd rather have "it" happen on set. The important thing is to walk through each character's journey with each actor, so that we both know what we want to accomplish. I have discovered a lot of talent through casting, because I treat the sessions as an opportunity to test our working relationship. Does an actor have lots of colours to play with, or are they rigid in some way? Can we connect? Is their ego in the way? Do they listen? Every actor needs something different from a director. Can I provide what they need to do the best they can? I want to know that the actor and I can work one-on-one, openly. That requires a confidence in each other that is ready to respond.

I like to keep things fresh. On set I often work with each actor separately so that the other actors don't necessarily know what is going to

Anne on the set of *Cowboys Don't Cry* after the bulls got loose and the crew took off after them.

happen—they will have to react to what is new. I make secret adjustments, which ups the stakes and results in a wonderful sense of surprise, sometimes igniting a whole new take on the scene. It keeps the performers—and the crew—in the moment. If people are confined by some plan and are reluctant to change, they will be discombobulated.

Thompson Final images are so critical to the meanings of films. Tell me about designing the final moments of *Bye Bye Blues*.

Wheeler In the story, it's early in the morning and Daisy gets up to see the band that she has grown with, musically, throughout the war, leave town for what will likely be an exciting future. The man who has encouraged her, taught her, loved her is also on that bus, and the urge to be a part of what they have brought together is overwhelming.

So many stories about war are about men doing the right thing. Rarely do we see the flip side, the decisions made by those outside the fighting. What Daisy does was a heroic act. The title, and the song "Bye Bye Blues," is a farewell to a part of her which leaves on that bus, a part of her that we will never know. To be honest we shot a couple of scenes that were scripted, and would have played after the final scene that is now in the movie. But they were redundant and dropped after the first rough cut.

Thompson Where did *Bye Bye Blues* premiere?

Wheeler In Edmonton! I brought my mother. I never talked to her about the film. She didn't want to read the script, to meet Rebecca Jenkins, to come on set or to the editing room. She did, however, come to a recording studio and play for hours with some of her old friends, and that music was a template for the style of music that drives the film. It's lively and uplifting, even when the words are rather melancholy. George Blondheim embraced the style, even sat down and played four-handed piano with her—which she thought was terrific. When I told her I was going to make a film about her, it amused her. "You better add a little spice to the story," she advised me. "A story about someone waiting could be quite boring." I reassured her that I'd add a little flavour. She never asked how much.

> So many stories about war are about men doing the right thing. Rarely do we see the flip side, the decisions made by those outside the fighting.

So when the film was going to be shown for the first time, we dressed to the nines and went together. I was terrified. Over a thousand people. I don't think she knew what to expect, maybe she thought it would be like *A War Story*. During the screening she was still, quiet, and I thought, "Oh no, what have I done? Maybe she is horrified!" Daisy, the lead character in the film, has a relationship with a man she grows to love, a father that disapproves, a life that is titillating. When the film ended, the hometown crowd went wild. I got her to stand up and folks cheered enthusiastically, and still she said nothing. After the audience left, I found a moment alone to ask her, "What did you think, Mom?" and she turned to me and privately asked, "How did you know all that?" Now that's drama.

Thompson The next year you pulled up your roots and moved to the West Coast. How did that move change your work?

Wheeler To be honest, it disconnected me artistically for a while. I had been driven by my roots and still had stories from Alberta to tell. The move was motivated for reasons other than my work. In BC you had Sandy Wilson with *My American Cousin*, Phil Borsos with *Grey Fox*, you and Sharon McGowan had done *The Lotus Eaters*. There were filmmakers telling stories out here, this place, as I had done on the Prairies, but I didn't belong. I no longer had my own library of stories—or sense of purpose. I moved from being an auteur, writing and directing my stories, to a director for hire and started to do more television. Maybe the change was good for me.

And thank goodness the work found me. I was offered the opportunity to tell stories that fed me, inspired me like *The Diviners*, *The War Between Us*, and *Mother Trucker*. These were mostly driven by television and I came to realize that television can be a great forum—and reach a huge audience.

Thompson Our collaboration in 1999 on *Better Than Chocolate* [I wrote and co-produced with Sharon McGowan] began with a phone call. When I'd finished the screenplay Sharon and I talked about you as the director. We had both seen all your films, and admired them and admired

> I came to realize that television can be a great forum—and reach a huge audience.

you as a leader in Canadian film. We thought you'd be brilliant with comedy. But we wondered if an established director would be interested in a lesbian romantic comedy. What made you want to come on board?

Wheeler The humour! And *Chocolate*'s theme of liberation is part of the continuum of stories I'd been telling about relationships between people, not only women. It was about tolerance and the power of understanding the other. These are themes I've always been drawn to but *Chocolate* offered me an opportunity to go back to comedy and to reach a new audience.

> *Chocolate*'s theme of liberation is part of the continuum of stories I'd been telling about relationships between people, not only women.

Thompson So here you were working with a writer and producer you hadn't worked with before.

Wheeler I was being invited to join a family rather than initiate one, yes. It was more your story than mine and that made the relationship to the story different. With *Bye Bye Blues* the project had stemmed from a personal place. You and Sharon had clear ideas of what a director was and what you were looking for in a collaborator. I remember being "auditioned." I always feel that auditions are a two-way street, and so it was with us. When I got the part, and it all came together, I felt excited.

Thompson During pre-production we did a lot of research.

Wheeler Yes, I had to get inside the heads of a generation and a community different from my own. You had gathered together a group of twelve or so young lesbians who were willing to tell us their stories, which gave me confidence. I worry about telling other people's stories. They also told us what kind of film they wanted to see. They didn't want the "poor me" film about coming out, feeling alienated—the full-of-angst film. They wanted a sexy movie that would make them laugh and feel good about themselves.

Thompson Let's talk about the script a bit. I recall we did a great deal of bouncing ideas off each other, and we did a draft together and continued to shape the script even when we were shooting.

Wheeler Happily, I was brought in early and we were all open to taking risks. The film in itself was a risk and that was exciting. Really it still is

quite unlike any other film out there. You provided the situation, and I found a way to execute it—in nineteen days! The fact that it was a "lesbian" story was neither here or there. I came from comedy; during university I had paid my way by doing musical comedy and theatre, so I was thrilled to get back to what I felt was a basic instinct. I concentrated on pacing the movie up, and playing with the unpredictable.

Thompson I've noticed that you have an impeccable plan when you shoot, but you're able to invent and develop on set with input and collaboration. You stay true to your vision but involve the talents around you.

Wheeler Yes, with the body-painting, for example. It could have been more conservative, more controlled. But I wanted it to be organic. [This scene is a visual feast, where the two young women paint each other's naked bodies.] The lighting, the possibilities were premeditated, but I let the actors paint what they felt like painting. When they needed a little

Christina Cox and Karen Dwyer from *Better Than Chocolate.* Photo by Rosamond Norbury.

> It's not so much about making a movie for the sake of making a movie—it's about what I will learn or perceive and what will others learn through me.

Wendy Crewsen with toys in *Better Than Chocolate*. Photo by Rosamond Norbury.

inspiration, I'd throw in an idea and they would take it a step further. It was a little like playing jazz. We could have pencilled on the bodies and had them fill in the lines, but I gave them the tune, the colours, and let them improvise creatively.

Thompson The shoot was nineteen days. That's hard.

Wheeler We were lucky that we had a lot of filmmakers on the producing team and on the crew. If I wanted input, I could turn to someone, and they would contribute.

Thompson I know that I was very nervous when we were invited to the Berlin Film Festival to premiere the film. Were you?

Wheeler I had no idea how people would react to the movie. Germany has a highly developed aesthetic sense of cinema. And we were competing against films that cost fifty times more than ours did. We had limited promotion and launching support. Yes, I was nervous. But we got this huge response—a wild screening with a standing ovation. And they got every joke! In fact, I think they "got" the film more than many North American audiences. The interviews were provocative and insightful.

Thompson As a director, what do you change in your approach between comedy and drama?

Wheeler Comedies like this one are bigger and more exaggerated than life. So while I want to keep it real so there's an emotional attachment for the audience, I torque things up. You can't play comedy only for realism, you have to bring the audience into the humour. The shape remains the same ... like a symphony, a dance, the act of making love.... You start by intriguing the audience, pulling them in closer, and engaging them—and hopefully they will embrace you and respond.

Thompson Once you've got the script, how do you start?

Wheeler I read the script many, many times so I can verbally walk through the whole story. Once I have a good grasp of it I start to plan out the shots, aware of the transitions. It's important to figure out what will pull me from one scene to the next. I think of each scene as a mini-play or a musical phrase, with a beginning, middle, and end. I design a lot of scenes in one shot, which means I choose where to be wide or tight, the pacing and so on within the scene. It's like editing before you shoot. In some scenes I may want lots of shots, which I can cut in a rhythm so I have to make sure I have all the bits and pieces I need. If possible, I spend a lot of time with my D.O.P. and designer and we're all clear before the shoot begins. Sometimes my plans are difficult to illustrate—I don't use storyboards. Usually I use floorplans—and my own notation, which includes everything from the size of lens, the sound, a sense of lighting, colours, and how the piece rises and falls, much like a complex piece of music. Directing is akin to conducting and I try to have it all in my head before I take the podium.

Thompson What directors have influenced you?

Wheeler I began making films as an art form because of the power they wielded. Film was a political tool used for change. I was influenced by the early filmmakers at the National Film Board, like Norman McLaren, Donald Brittain, and Colin Low, and cinema verité auteurs

> Directing is akin to conducting and I try to have it all in my head before I take the podium.

such as Frederick Wiseman. Then when I moved into drama I watched directors like John Cassavetes who were breaking the mould, and internationals like Satyajit Ray, who revealed worlds outside of my own experience. Recently, I have been moved by the work of Fernando Meirelles and his ability to capture reality.

Thompson What keeps you going?

Wheeler It's not so much about making a movie for the sake of making a movie—it's about what I will learn or perceive and what will others learn through me. With *Bye Bye Blues* I learned a lot about myself by putting myself in Daisy's place. She chose to stay and nurture her family, which in some ways parallels my decision to stay in Canada. *Better Than Chocolate* plunged me into issues of gender and made me more aware of the spectrum of what is masculine and feminine.

Thompson Any regrets?

Wheeler Not really. Sometimes I think I would have made bigger more marketable films if I'd gone to the States early in my career but I am aware that there would have been trade-offs. Sometimes I haven't fought hard enough for my work, or taken a big enough risk artistically. Mostly I think I've been so lucky to have had this opportunity to explore and express.

■

THE DEAD

Jean-Claude Lauzon

JEAN-CLAUDE LAUZON interviewed by **Claude Racine*** translated and with notes by **Jim Leach**

* Originally published in French in *24 Images*, no. 61 (Summer 1992).

■

Racine How did you create the story of *Léolo*?

Lauzon I began to write when I was in Sicily for *Un zoo la nuit*. Everything started from texts that I had written when I was young. The first line that I put down on paper was, I think: "The odours and the light that have welded my first thoughts together." Then quietly, the mother grafted herself on, then the brother, the relationship with the "pals." The first draft consisted more of images and ideas which ceaselessly returned, like an obsession. I take many notes, they accumulate, and slowly I begin to find connections between things that did not have them before. Some things drop out, others become more and more strong. Little by little, the film ends up imposing itself. It is not something that I decide, as if I said that I was going to deal with such and such a theme. I would be incapable of providing a synopsis for Telefilm or Sogic before beginning to write my screenplay. The story is now very structured, but that came afterwards.

All that has stayed with me from *Un zoo la nuit* is the scene where the guy washes his father. When I began to write *Léolo*, I said to myself I would like to succeed in making a film in which there would be the same lyricism and poetry without being obliged to pass through the explanatory side that there was in that film; that is to say, the dramatic plot, the villains, the good guys, the money, the crime thriller. What was most important for me was to be able to move from one situation to another while maintaining the same intensity. That is the only thing I knew before I started writing.

Racine You refer to *Un zoo la nuit* but *Léolo* has more in common with your short film *Piwi*.

Lauzon That is very true. *Léolo* is much closer to *Piwi* at the level of tone, for example. Besides, *Un zoo* was just an interlude. When I decided to make this film, two ways were open to me: that of *Piwi* and that of the mainstream, the more popular cinema as defined by "the film guys," as in *Un zoo*. In fact, I have the impression that *Léolo* is my first real film. The others were like juggling with different elements. Now, I am beginning to better understand what interests me.

Racine Several scenes in *Léolo* suggest that, despite all that is said to the contrary, it is possible in Quebec to depict almost any kind of subject in films; that the obstacles are in the heads of the screenwriters.

Lauzon We are very spoiled in Quebec. There are far too many filmmakers complaining because they imagine the institutions will prevent them from filming certain things. It must be said that in my case, *Un zoo* helped a lot, and people were afraid to criticize me. On the other hand, I was completely forgotten between the two films, as if I no longer existed. But when I came back with a project, I was very well received. I can no longer listen to the speeches of the Quebec filmmakers who tell me they are all unknown geniuses and their projects are too creative for the institutions to understand them. That's bullshit! You can do what you want here as a director, if you have the drive to defend your project, if you are capable of beating down the doors. If you don't believe enough in your project, that's your problem. Many people talk of censorship by the institutions—that's a complete joke!

Racine But there is also TV. Radio-Québec, for example, is involved with your film. The representatives of TV intervene during the different stages of production, including screenings during the editing.

Lauzon If a film is modified because of television, it is exclusively the fault of the director. That is sorted out when the representatives of TV want to enter the editing room! If you are soft enough to let them in, that's your problem. Don't start shouting afterwards that you haven't made the film you wanted! In life, it is never the fault of others when you don't have something. Quebec is one of the most free countries in the world in terms of expression and creativity. What is most important is to have 20 per cent creativity and 80 per cent drive. You must be capable of pushing, and when someone offers a "script doctor" to you, if you decide you don't want one and they say, "You won't make your film," you must have the dignity to not make your film. It may be that Radio-Canada is serious when they say to someone: "If you don't do such and such, we won't give you the money." They certainly refused my film, and it was Radio-Québec that finally bought it. If someone said that to

> You can do what you want here as a director, if you have the drive to defend your project, if you are capable of beating down the doors. If you don't believe enough in your project, that's your problem.

me, I couldn't care less; I wouldn't make the film and that's all. There are other things in life besides cinema that interest me, and I think that not being afraid to lose my "job" remains one of my greatest strengths. I'm not looking for a "job" as a director. To be sure, if TV hires you for a series such as *Montréal, ville ouverte*,[1] you won't pass that up … I have also had an extraordinary opportunity to earn my living in publicity. For *Léolo*, many people at the NFB said to me: "You'll see when the French producers come on board, they will censor you." However, you will ask if anyone tried to tell me what to do. The French producers tried to make me cast Pierre Richard.[2] If you go down on your knees before a producer because the gentleman is very rich, you will never make the film you want. I repeat, a director is always responsible for his film.

Racine Is it because you take the time to do things as you want them that there was a five-year gap between *Un zoo la nuit* and *Léolo*?

Lauzon That's part of the reason, to the extent that between the two I would have had the chance, for example, of going to work in Los Angeles, but I told myself that I didn't make *Un zoo la nuit* to find myself with a "boss" in Los Angeles. I would like to work there under good conditions, but it would be impossible for me to make a film like *Bethune* and to have a star like Sutherland as my "boss."[3]

Racine But isn't that also what gives you your reputation, when they say that you have an impossible temperament?

Lauzon Those who say that don't know me very well. I have got on well with all the heads of department with whom I have worked. There is one thing, however, that I never let myself accept, that we are in Quebec and the reality here will not allow us to do such and such a thing.… If someone begins to talk to me that way, I am capable of breaking the place up. When I make a film, I do not judge myself against what is being done here; I think of the cinema of Wenders, Godard, and Bertolucci. It is at the international level that the competition must take place. For me, every time one judges a film that aspires to a professional quality, it must be weighed against contemporary cinema, and the cinema at this time is Spike Lee and David Lynch. We must stop looking among our-

> If you go down on your knees before a producer because he is very rich, you will never make the film you want. A director is always responsible for his film.

selves and asking ourselves if our film is better than the latest Beaudin or the latest Simoneau.[4] That is not the level that matters!

Racine Where does the world that we find in your film come from? It seems to be in large part autobiographical.

Lauzon It is a big lie based on a truth. If, for example, the father in *Un zoo* is compared to the one in *Léolo*, they are two completely different characters. Yet I had only one father. I have never had neighbours like the ones in the film, my grandfather did not live with us, I never tried to kill him, I have never been in love with an Italian neighbour. That's fiction. Certainly there are real connections at the level of emotions, but what matters is knowing how to make these personal hang-ups universal. If not, it is unlikely to move people.

Racine The young Léo Lozeau takes refuge in the imagination to the point that he wants to change his name to Léolo Lozone—

Lauzon I wanted my film to be a kind of homage to dream. We knew the epoch of Brel and Bob Dylan when the arts and poetry carried a much greater weight. Today we seem to be in a world where power belongs to merchants, lawyers, and accountants. So I wanted to make a film that paid homage to creativity. That is why the young boy always functions on the basis of his imagination, and his social reality is secondary. I don't want to disown the Québécois, I am only saying that *Léolo* does not have the flag draped all over it, that he has only to open his cupboard to be somewhere else.

Racine It is difficult to stop oneself seeing an analogy to the Quebec situation in this film.

Lauzon I know that many people are already beginning to talk of *Léolo* as a pre-referendum film.[5] Because of, among other things, the little Québécois who, in the film, does body-building for ten years to return to confront the anglophone who punched him in the face and, when he finds himself in front of him, he is afraid and drops his fists. It is a nice big symbol, except that it is important to know that there was no question at the beginning, in the screenplay, that he would be an anglophone. He was simply your typical loudmouth such as one often meets

> I wanted my film to be a kind of homage to dream. We knew the epoch of Brel and Bob Dylan when the arts and poetry carried a much greater weight.

in the alleys. It was purely by chance—even if you will tell me that there is no such thing as chance—because we could not find a typical loud-mouth among the francophone actors. So I decided to return to Lorne[6] with whom I had worked in *Un zoo la nuit*. When they see that Bourgault[7] is in my film, there will certainly be political interpretations, but I assure you that there was absolute nothing calculated about this choice.

Racine How did you choose the musical pieces?

Lauzon I spent two years searching for the music. I must say that when I write, I fall into a strange state: I stop working, I sit down to read for a while, I listen to many songs that interest me. In the screenplay, every-thing was written to music: Tom Waits as much as the religious music at the beginning, or that of Sister Marie Keyrouz. I had someone in a music store who searched for music for me. He would call me to say that he had found an Arab disc, for example, or something very special.

Racine Did you want to make the imaginary scenes more comprehen-sible and clear by pairing them with certain music?

Lauzon It was rather a desire for lyricism than a desire for efficiency. It was not at all to aid comprehension. For example, the scene in which we see Ginette Reno[8] sitting on the toilet with a turkey: when you place the music of Thomas Tallis over that, along with the play of light, it makes the scene more sacred instead of making it vulgar—because that could have been in very bad taste. The music gives it a kind of aura.

Racine How are these pieces integrated into the film? Did you seek a mu-sical development?

Lauzon Yes. For example, the music of the Stones at the end begins with the choir, and someone who has forgotten this song might believe that it is the music of Thomas Tallis or Ariel Ramirez once again, and gradually you notice that it is the Stones. I very much liked the idea of that transition. The Stones song is for me not only a rock 'n' roll song. Besides, these songs all have something sacred for me. I am, certainly, not especially religious, but it really helps me create. I very much like the idea that the despair of those youths becomes apparent in the phrase of the Stones that says, "You Can't Always Get What You Want," as in

> In the screenplay, everything was written to music: Tom Waits as much as the reli-gious music at the beginning, or that of Sister Marie Keyrouz.

the sequence with Ti-cul Godin and the cat; that music absolutely gets to me.

Racine The rights to the Stones music must have been very expensive.

Lauzon Yes, it cost a lot, but it was very clear before signing with the producers—all the music was written into the initial screenplay—that I wanted this music and if they were not able to provide it, we would forget the film. There was only one Italian song that we were not able to get because the singer had decided he would never sell the rights. For music like that of Sister Marie Keyrouz or the Stones, it was easier to negotiate because the big companies have their offices in New York, whereas for the Italian, because he was not a major singer, it was complicated to find out who really owned the rights. I was lucky to be working with Lyse Lafontaine as producer, and Lyse spoiled me a lot because a film from here has never acquired music like that of the Stones.

Racine Excrement has a great importance for the Lozeaus. How did this element impose itself?

Lauzon It is an image that I have retained from infancy, and it is connected to the mother, but I can't explain any more than that where the idea comes from. Where did this or that canvas of Picasso come from? At a given moment, certain things take possession of you and you want to express them. I took no pleasure in showing it. This element took the proportions it has in the film without my asking myself where it came from; it is there and that's all.

Racine In fact, this element brings all the members of the family together—

Lauzon I wanted the film to be very sensual, at the level of smells, of the comfort from the mother—as in the scene where Léolo is in the arms of his mother. It is for that I cast Ginette: I wanted a big mother.

Racine How did you cast the actors?

Lauzon Many people imagine that I absolutely wanted to cast non-professional actors, but that is not the case. I would have preferred to work with real actors, professionals, if I had been able to find them. It was only that they did not exist for these kinds of roles. I absolutely wanted

> I wanted the film to be very sensual, at the level of smells, of the comfort from the mother—as in the scene where Léolo is in the arms of his mother.

a body-builder; for fat women, you have the choice of three in Quebec. At the beginning, Ginette thought that it was the star I wanted. I had to make clear that I was calling on her as an actress, to play the role of the mother, and that it was not a question of her singing or performing over the credits. But despite everything, I am very lucky with my actors. I still ask myself why Roger Le Bel[9] agreed to be in *Un zoo la nuit* or why Ginette Reno agreed to sit on the toilet.

Racine The children in *Léolo* are very different from those we usually see in cinema. I am thinking, among others, of the sequence in which they dare Ti-cul Godin to "screw" the cat.

Lauzon Rock Demers[10] will certainly find that very rough!

Racine What is it like directing children?

> You tell the children in precise detail how to look, how to hold their bodies and shoulders, and they reproduce what you have told them, but they do not give you any surprises. It's like modelling rather than directing: you play with their bodies, physical lies.

Lauzon These children bring their own experiences. It is very difficult to work with them. They ask you what to do, you tell them in precise detail, how to look, how to hold their bodies and shoulders, and they reproduce what you have told them, but they do not give you any surprises. It's like modelling rather than directing: you play with their bodies, physical lies.

Racine How is the real connected to the imaginary? There is an organic link here with *L'avalée des avalés*,[11] which the worm tamer is reading: the imaginary and reality become confused with each other. You were probably conscious of this when you were writing.

Lauzon I read *L'avalée des avalés* during a strange period in my life, and I had never returned to it. What I remembered above all from this book was the very beautiful sentence that the boy recites at the beginning of the film: "All I ask of a book is that it should inspire me with courage, inspire me with energy, inspire me with the urgent need to act." And I found that that this is precisely what this book contains. When I find a good book, it becomes something of a launching pad; it stimulates me as a creator.

Racine You pay a kind of homage to André Petrowski incarnated in the character of the worm tamer played by Pierre Bourgault.

Lauzon It was André Petrowski[12] who inspired this character, but it was enormously transposed. My relationship with him was much more concrete. He began by making me read novels, took me to the theatre, showed me the editing rooms at the NFB; he read some of my writing and put me in touch with people in the creative world to try to stimulate me to write. In the film, he has almost become a wise old man or an angel. We realize at the end that he is a character who, with his collections of books and all sorts of objects, has passed through time, through history, helping artists. He does not even meet the boy. It is a relationship transposed into the imaginary, as if it is communicated solely through thought. There is not one shot where they are together.

Racine Does the fact of having shot commercials help you in making films?

Lauzon Enormously! It helped me a great deal by giving me the concrete experience of being on a set. I have worked with Italians, with Frenchmen, and that brings a foreign perspective to reassure you that your way of seeing things is worthwhile. Shooting commercials also speeded up my evolution with regard to composition. I no longer look through a camera lens in the same way.

Racine But making a theatrical film and making a commercial do not involve the same kind of shots.

Lauzon It is absolutely not the same kind of shots or compositions; it is a different language. Extreme long shots have no place in TV. But, on the other hand, commercials have the advantage of allowing you to try certain technical things. When you are a film student and have had no experience, you don't know what it means to ask for a hundred-foot dolly shot. But when you direct a film professionally and you have made commercials, you can perhaps treat yourself to one, but you know that it will need the guys to set it up and make it level, there will need to be parking for the trucks, etc. It removes completely the abstract idea of only seeing a camera to move it. If you know what it means to ask for such and such a shot, you can stick to it, but you can also plan your day and let technique take its place below certain important factors, like the quality of the acting, for example. In other words, advertising is a big

He began by making me read novels, took me to the theatre, showed me the editing rooms at the NFB; he read some of my writing and put me in touch with people in the creative world to try to stimulate me to write.

"plaything" for teaching how to work, which also means knowing how to cope with stress, how to convince other people to accept your ideas. But it is above all how to fight, because to shoot a feature film is also a battle at every moment.

Racine How do you work with the different members of the crew, such as the sound technician, the editor, or the cinematographer? Do you give them directions or leave them a great deal of latitude?

Lauzon Guy Dufaux[13] and I have worked together so much that we are moving in the same direction. We have made discoveries by trying out all sorts of things in commercials, including the Bell Canada campaigns where we had large budgets. We would look at the rushes afterwards; there were things that we liked, others that we liked less. We would gradually get a more precise idea of the light and the tone we wanted to give our film. There was also a very close collaboration with François Séguin, the artistic director, François Barbeau, the costume designer, and Jacques Benoît, my assistant director to whom I owe a great deal. Once the film had been edited, all five of us viewed it shot by shot, listening to the opinion of each department head, and we completed the editing together. It is really good to be able to collaborate to such a degree, because normally, at this stage, they are no longer there and you finish the film alone with the editor.

Racine With regard to the allusions? I am thinking of the fishing scene, for example, where we see Jacques Marcotte with whom Forcier[14] writes his screenplays. One could also make a connection between the little boy who Italianizes his name and Félix Cotnoir in *Kalamazoo* who wants to be known as Felichiano Montenegro.

Lauzon I did not want to allude to Marc-André at all, although he is a filmmaker whom I really love a great deal and to whom I feel very close. When I was younger, I watched his films and said to myself that these were the kind of films that I would like to make. With regard to Marcotte, he found himself there by chance. The fishing scene takes place in a world that I have known because the place seen in the film is where I would go to fish.

Advertising is a big "plaything" for teaching how to work, which also means knowing how to cope with stress, how to convince other people to accept your ideas. But it is above all how to fight, because to shoot a feature film is also a battle at every moment.

Racine Why is the family gripped by madness?

Lauzon I felt that it was a good idea that the character should be further compelled to think differently; because there is no melancholy with regard to that madness. In any case, where is the line between creativity and mental illness? This is simply a family of "trippers," but they trip out over different things.

Racine But at the end, Léolo is also carried off.

Lauzon I don't think he becomes mad like the rest of the family, nor do I believe that he departs unhappily because there are no signs of degradation in the course of the film. The fuse goes and he surrenders in order to abandon himself to the imaginary, and that is why *L'avalée des avalés* returns in what he has written: "And I will go to rest my head between two words in the valley of the vanquished." For me, it is rather a liberation. The worm tamer is smiling at the end. What was important is not the boy's body, not his temporal death, but what he leaves behind in his writings. I did not want it to be too "heavy," which explains the choice of upbeat music rather than "down." That little boy represents for me the reign of the power of the imagination.

Racine The form and structure of *Léolo* are not as conventional as they were in *Un zoo*. Did you ask yourself about how the audience would react?

Lauzon I believe that *Léolo* would have been much less noticed if it had been released at the time when we were going to see the films of Lina Wertmüller or Fassbinder. It is becoming difficult to see a film where there is a point of view and, especially, a point of view that does not defend a cause. Many people today like a film because it defends a noble cause: feminism, anti-racism, etc. I can't wait to see how these people will react because this is not at all a fashionable film; it is a bit of a dinosaur film in which there is a kind of thought that is very far from us today.

I was really lucky to have the chance to make the film I was thinking of. It is rather extraordinary, because today they are always looking for, as a result of television and the need for pre-sales, a story that is

> I was really lucky to have the chance to make the film I was thinking of.... Today they are always looking for a story that is readily comprehensible or at least that works according to a logic appropriate to our times.

readily comprehensible or at least that works according to a logic appropriate to our times.

Racine Finally, I remember telephoning you two years ago, when we were preparing a dossier on the 1980s and soliciting the participation of filmmakers who had made a mark in that decade, and you replied to me: "I have made only one feature film, I don't consider myself a filmmaker."

Lauzon I still don't consider myself a filmmaker. It is not that I am denying the reality, it is simply that the status of an artist is an extremely fragile status that you can lose in 24 hours. There are, for example, people who have done a great deal in their lives between seventeen and twenty-two, and afterwards they become good little bureaucrats. There is such a crowd here who consider themselves filmmakers! At that time, I had made only one feature; I was hiring myself out to make commercials, I was experiencing things that interested me, such as airplane flying and deep-sea diving. For me, an artist is someone like Gilles Maheu: he is a guy like a priest, who consecrates his life to his art. I truly believed, between the two films, that I would never make another film, nor do I know how many more times I am going to direct in my life. With regard to *Léolo*, I have only been fortunate enough to have the naïveté and determination to see the idea through. Today the film is finished, and I am happy, but I will pass on to something else. I am going back on the road to do the other things that interest me and perhaps, in three, four, or five years, an idea will come to me. But as long as I feel good about it, and as long as I feel strong enough not to have to write, I will do other things with my life.

> For me, an artist is like a priest, who consecrates his life to his art.

NOTES

1. *Montréal, ville ouverte* was a popular miniseries broadcast on Radio-Canada in 1992. It dealt with investigations into organized crime in Montreal in the 1950s.

2. Pierre Richard is a French actor and the star of many farcical comedies since the 1960s.

3. Donald Sutherland starred as the title character in *Bethune: The Making of a Hero* (1990), an epic Canadian film about Norman Bethune, the doctor who became a national hero in China during the 1930s.

4. Jean Beaudin and Yves Simoneau are veteran Québécois film directors.

5. *Léolo* was released in 1992, just as the debate leading up to the second referendum on Quebec sovereignty, to be held in 1995, was getting under way.

6. *Un zoo la nuit* was the first feature film for Lorne Brass, a Canadian actor who has enjoyed a long career. He appeared also in *Bethune*.

7. Pierre Bourgault, journalist, academic, and Parti Québécois politician.

8. Ginette Reno is a popular singer who has had many hits in Quebec and who acted in film for the first time in *Léolo*. She has appeared in several important roles since.

9. Roger Le Bel is a respected Quebec actor. *Un zoo la nuit* was his last film.

10. Rock Demers is a Quebec producer responsible for the successful series of children's films *Tales for All*.

11. *The Swallower Swallowed* (1966) was the poetic novel by Réjean Ducharme that sparks Léo's imagination after the worm tamer leaves a copy in his home.

12. André Petrowski was the producer at the National Film Board who befriended Lauzon and inspired him to become a filmmaker.

13. Guy Dufaux is a cinematographer, born in France, who has worked on many important Quebec films since the 1960s.

14. Marc-André Forcier, a major Quebec film director whose films have their roots in surrealism and who was known as the *enfant terrible* of Quebec cinema until the media decided Lauzon was an even greater nuisance.

FEATURE FILMS

GARY BURNS

A Problem with Fear (2003)   Director, writer
waydowntown (2000)   Producer, director, writer
Kitchen Party (1997)   Director, writer
The Suburbanators (1995)   Director, writer

TRENT CARLSON

Fido (2006)   Co-producer
The Delicate Art of Parking (2003)   Director, writer

BLAKE CORBET

Fido (2006)   Producer
Missing in America (2005)   Co-producer
The Delicate Art of Parking (2003)   Producer, writer
Mile Zero (2001)   Producer

ANDREW CURRIE

Fido (2006)   Director, writer
The Delicate Art of Parking (2003)   Producer
Mile Zero (2001)   Director

MICHAEL DOWSE

It's All Gone Pete Tong (2004)   Director, writer
FUBAR (2002)   Producer, director, writer, cinematographer, editor
Bad Money (1999)   Editor

JEAN-CLAUDE LAUZON

Léolo (1992) Director, writer
Un zoo la nuit (1987) Director, writer

GUY MADDIN

Brand Upon the Brain (2006) Director, writer
The Saddest Music in the World (2003) Director, writer
Twilight of the Ice Nymphs (1997) Director
Careful (1992) Director, writer, cinematographer
Archangel (1990) Director, writer, cinematographer
Tales from the Gimli Hospital (1988) Director, writer, cinematographer

MINA SHUM

Long Life, Happiness and Prosperity (2002) Executive Producer,
    director, writer
Drive, She Said (1997) Director, writer
Double Happiness (1994) Director, writer

LYNNE STOPKEWICH

Suspicious River (2000) Director, writer
Kissed (1996) Producer, director, writer, editor

ANNE WHEELER

Edge of Madness (2002) Director, writer
Suddenly Naked (2001) Executive Producer, director
Marine Life (2000) Director
Better Than Chocolate (1999) Director
The War Between Us (1995) Director
Angel Square (1990) Director, writer
Bye Bye Blues (1989) Producer, director, writer
Cowboys Don't Cry (1988) Associate producer, director
Loyalties (1986) Director, writer
A War Story (1981) Producer, director, writer

For further information go to www.imdb.com.

BART BEATY is an associate professor in the Faculty of Communication and Culture at the University of Calgary. He is the author of *Fredric Wertham and the Critique of Mass Culture* (University Press of Mississippi, 2005), *Unpopular Culture: Transforming the European Comic Book in the 1990s* (University of Toronto Press, 2006), and, with Rebecca Sullivan, *Canadian Television Today* (University of Calgary Press, 2006). His monograph, *David Cronenberg's A History of Violence*, is the inaugural book in the Canadian Cinema series published by the University of Toronto Press (forthcoming, 2008).

JIM LEACH is a professor in the Department of Communication, Popular Culture and Film at Brock University. His publications include *Claude Jutra, Filmmaker* (McGill-Queen's University Press, 1999) and *British Film* (Cambridge University Press, 2004). He is also the author (with Louis Giannetti) of *Understanding Movies* (fourth Canadian edition) (Pearson, 2005) and co-editor (with Jeannette Sloniowski) of *Candid Eyes: Essays on Canadian Documentaries* (University of Toronto Press, 2003). His most recent book is *Film in Canada* (Oxford University Press, 2006).

JACQUELINE LEVITIN is a filmmaker and film historian–critic who teaches at Simon Fraser University in Vancouver. Her recent film work has been in ethnographic documentary ("Building Bridge: A Housing

Project for Women" [2003]), live video collaborations for dance and theatre, and an experimental documentary, *Mahjong & Chicken Feet* (2008), on China's relation with her Jewish "others." She is the co-editor of *Women Filmmakers: Refocusing* (2003), a dialogue between women filmmakers, critics, and theorists.

GEORGE MELNYK is an associate professor of Canadian Studies and Film Studies, Faculty of Communication and Culture, at the University of Calgary. His publications on cinema include One *Hundred Years of Canadian Cinema* (2004), *My Mother Is an Alien: Ten Takes on Life and Film* (2004), and *Great Canadian Film Directors* (2007). He is currently completing a monograph on urbanity in Canadian cinema and organizing the second volume of this series.

KALLI PAAKSPUU teaches at York University and is a Genie-winning filmmaker, new media, and theatre artist. Her dissertation, "Rhetorics of Colonialism in Visual Documentation" (University of Toronto), examines early cross-cultural communication and the dialogical storytelling on both sides of the camera. Her publications and art projects specialize in visual, oral, and mnemonic knowledge practices. She is developing a feature-film musical based on Liliane Atlan's play *Les Mers Rouges*, about the Sephardic Jews' exodus from Spain, after directing a successful English world premiere at Toronto's Fringe Festival in 2005.

PEGGY THOMPSON is an associate professor in the Creative Writing Program at the University of British Columbia. She is the screenwriter of the feature films *The Lotus Eaters* (1993), for which she won a Genie Award for Best Screenplay, and *Better Than Chocolate*. She was one of the producers on the feature film *Saint Monica* (2002) and most recently was one of the executive producers on the documentary *The Oldest Basketball Team in the World* (2006).

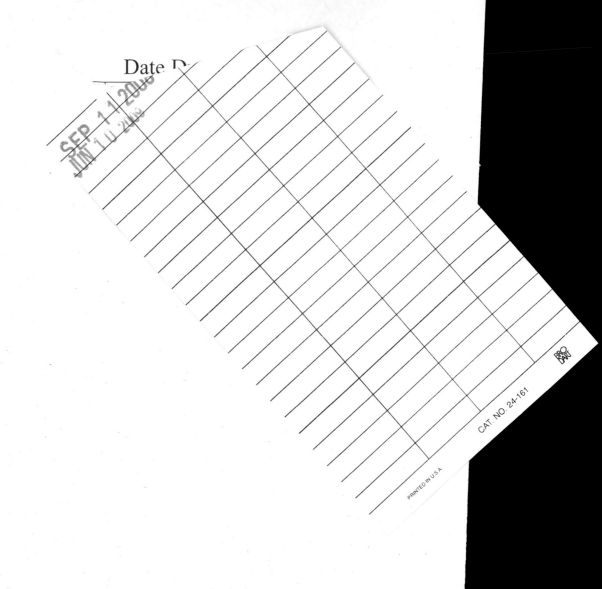

Date D

PRINTED IN U.S.A.

CAT. NO. 24-161

BRO
DART